The Heart of Worship
Studies in the Psalms

The Heart of

Worship

Studies in the Psalms

Lee Roy Martin

The Heart of Worship
Studies in the Psalms

Copyright © 2011 Lee Roy Martin. All rights reserved.

To My Students

Lee Roy Martin holds the Doctor of Theology degree in Old Testament from the University of South Africa. He also has a B.A. in Biblical Studies from Lee University and a M.Div. from the Pentecostal Theological Seminary. In addition to his degrees, he studied biblical languages for three years at Mid-America Baptist Theological Seminary. He has served 27 years as a pastor in the Church of God and now is Professor of Old Testament and Biblical Languages at the Pentecostal Theological Seminary in Cleveland, TN USA, where he teaches a course on the Book of Psalms. He also serves as Editor of the *Journal of Pentecostal Theology*. He has taught Seminary extension courses at the Universidad Teológica del Caribe in Puerto Rico, Han Young University in Seoul, Korea, and the Asian Seminary of Christian Ministries in Manila, Philippines.

❧ CONTENTS ❧

Introduction:
How to Study the Psalms

Psalm 23

[1] The Lord is my shepherd; I shall not want.
[2] He maketh me to lie down in green pastures:
    he leadeth me beside the still waters.
[3] He restoreth my soul:
    he leadeth me in the paths of righteousness
    for his name's sake.
[4] Yea, though I walk through the valley of the shadow of death,
    I will fear no evil:
    for thou art with me; thy rod and thy staff they comfort me.
[5] Thou preparest a table before me
    in the presence of mine enemies:
    thou anointest my head with oil; my cup runneth over.
[6] Surely goodness and mercy shall follow me
    all the days of my life:
    and I will dwell in the house of the Lord for ever.

Psalm 23 is perhaps the most beloved chapter of the Bible, and it exemplifies the power of the book of Psalms. It uniquely captures the beauty and value of the believer's relationship to God. The psalm is simple yet profound. It is straightforward yet deep in meaning. It appeals both to children and to the aged, to the new believer and to the seasoned saint.

The book of Psalms is sometimes referred to as the songbook of Israel, and both Jews and Christians have consistently witnessed to the power of the Psalms to give voice to their prayers and their expressions of worship. The Psalms have this power because, unlike other parts of Scripture, they are not God's words directed towards Israel. The Psalms are Israel's words directed to God in worshipful and prayerful response to his presence and actions among them. As long as Christians continue to acknowledge God's presence and activity in the Church, the Psalms will serve as a meaningful expression of the Christian response to God in worship and prayer. The Psalms provide examples of prayer and worship, and they have much to say about our worship today.

The Psalms are lyric poetry and exhibit all of the features of poetry. The 150 Psalms were written by a variety of Hebrew authors over the span of several hundred years. The Psalms include several types of songs that vary considerably in style, content, and form. The Psalms are cited often in the New Testament, where many of them are associated with the life of Jesus the Messiah. The importance of the Psalms is illustrated further by their continued use throughout history both in public liturgy and in private devotions.

The Power of the Psalms

Songs of worship

The Psalms tell us that worship is deep, intense, and passionate. Worship flows out of the believer's relationship with God. Psalm 23 tells us that we can experience God in *personal relationship*: "The Lord is my shepherd". Yes, God is the great shepherd of the Church, but as the psalmist declares, he is "my" shepherd. As my shepherd, the Lord provides for my needs. As my shepherd, the Lord brings me to the green pastures where I can find rest. As my shepherd, the Lord leads me to a place of refreshing beside the still waters. As my shepherd, the Lord "restores my soul". When I walk in the dark valley, I do not fear because my shepherd walks with me to protect me. He strikes out with his rod against any enemy that might approach, and he stretches forth his staff to guide me and to pull me closer to himself. Because the Lord is my shepherd, I will worship him.

The Psalms tell us also that prayer is honest and fervent. In fact, the Psalms" honesty and fervency may at times seem harsh, especially on those occasions when the psalmist prayed for the violent destruction of enemies and their children (e.g. Psalm 3.7). These imprecatory psalms are difficult to reconcile with Christ's command to love our enemies. It should be remembered, however, that these psalms are cries for help, emerging from situations of deep suffering and oppression, and that the New Testament allows for God's intervention as vindicator of his people (Rom. 12.19; 1 Thess. 1.8; 2 Tim. 4.14; Heb. 10.30-31; Jude 14-15; Rev. 6.10).

Songs of faith

The diversity of experiences that we find in the Psalms testifies to a dynamic life of faith. Psalm 23 teaches us to believe that "goodness and mercy" will follow us, all the days of our lives. It shows us the importance of dwelling in the "house of the Lord forever".

At first glance, we may view the Psalms as songs of praise only, but we find other types of songs as well. In the Psalms we find passionate prayers—what scholars call the laments. We also find exalted praises—the hymns. The lament and the hymn are opposite poles of Christian experience. The prayers of lament speak to our times of great pain, and the hymns teach us to rejoice in times of great joy. The Psalms teach us that life is always moving, always changing, always developing. The Psalms demonstrate how to worship God even in the midst of these changes and movements.

Songs of instruction

Not only do the Psalms offer a model of worship, but they also instruct us in many other ways. The prayers for deliverance teach us about God's ability and willingness to save his people. God's acts of deliverance are mentioned in the thanksgiving Psalms and in the hymns. God's saving work includes his providential care, his forgiveness of sin, his healing of sickness, and his giving of his Spirit (Ps. 51.10-11). God is also portrayed powerfully as creator and sovereign of the universe. As king, God is enthroned in heaven, active on earth, and coming to reign over the world (Ps. 96). Therefore, we should worship him!

Songs of prophecy

The writers of the New Testament found in the Psalms many testimonies to Jesus Christ. Christians have viewed the Psalms as predictive of the birth, life, death, and teachings of Jesus. Jesus himself quoted from the Psalms many times, and in the entire New Testament we find over one hundred quotations from the Psalms. Portions of the Psalms that are commonly cited as Messianic include the following:

Ps. 2.1-2   Opposition to the Messiah

Ps. 2.7	The divinity of Jesus
Ps. 2.9	The rule of Jesus
Ps. 16.8-11	The resurrection of Jesus
Ps. 22	The crucifixion of Jesus
Ps. 31.5	The death of Jesus
Ps. 34.20	Jesus' bones not broken
Ps. 40.6-8	The faithfulness of Jesus
Ps. 41.9	Messiah betrayed by a friend
Ps. 69.4	The rejection of Jesus
Ps. 69.9	Jesus cleanses the temple
Ps. 78.2	Prediction of Jesus' use of parables
Ps. 110.1	The divinity of Jesus
Ps. 110.4	The eternal priesthood of Jesus
Ps. 118.22-23	Jesus as the cornerstone
Ps. 118.26	Triumphal entry of Jesus

The Book of Psalms

Many of the books in the Bible begin with an introductory statement. For example, the book of Isaiah starts out, "The vision of Isaiah, the son of Amos in the days of King Uzziah". It tells us who wrote it, what it is about, and when it was written. Unlike other books of the Bible, however, the book of Psalms has no statement of introduction. One reason that the book of Psalms does not have an introductory heading is because Psalms is not a book like other biblical books. It is not a book that was composed as a single document from beginning to end. Instead, it is a collection of songs that were brought together over a period of hundreds of years, beginning with a collection of David's psalms, with others added later. Psalm 137, for example, was written after the Babylonian captivity, several hundred years after the time of David. Psalm 137 remembers the days when the Israelites were in the land of Babylon, and the Babylonians asked them to sing a song from the land of Israel, but the Israelites hung their harps on the willows. They said, "How can we sing the song of the Lord in a strange land?" That was about 500 BC, and David lived about 1000 BC—a span of 500 years. Over this period of five hundred years the Psalms were put together. Therefore, it is not a book like the other books of the Bible; instead, it is a collection of individual songs.

The Five Books of Psalms

The book of Psalms is divided into five divisions, which are called the "Five Books". Book One consists of Psalms 1 through 41; Book Two is Psalms 42 through 72; Book Three is Psalms 73 through 89; Book Four is Psalms 90 through 106; and Book Five covers Psalms 107 through 150. The psalms in each of these five books were grouped together on account of similarities in topic, perspective, usage in worship, or authorship. Most of the psalms of David are in Books One and Two, but other psalms of David are scattered throughout the entire Psalter. The fivefold division of the Psalter may have been intended as a structural parallel to the five books of Moses.

The five books are marked off with a doxology that concludes sections 1, 2, 3, and 4. The doxologies are as follows:

Blessed be the Lord God of Israel from everlasting to everlasting. Amen and amen (Ps. 41.13).

Blessed be his glorious name forever and ever. Let the whole earth be filled with his glory. Amen and amen (Ps. 72.).

Blessed be the Lord forevermore. Amen (Ps. 89.).

Blessed be the Lord God of Israel from everlasting to everlasting, and let all the people say, "Amen, praise the Lord" (Ps. 106.).

Thus, these sections end with similar declarations of praise to the Lord. These doxologies are like links, holding the book together.

Authorship of the Psalms

When we think of the book of Psalms, we naturally think of them as the Psalms of David, but not all of them were written by David. Even Psalm 1, the very first psalm in the book, does not include the heading, "A Psalm of David". Psalm 1, along with many other psalms, does not include the name of the writer. Still, among the psalms that give the name of the author, David is credited with writing 73. Moses is named as the author of Psalm 90; Solomon wrote Psalms 72 and 127; Heman wrote Psalm 88; Ethan wrote Psalm 89; a group called "the sons of Korah" wrote eleven psalms (Pss. 42, 44-49, 84-85, 87-88); and another group called "the sons of Asaph" also wrote eleven Psalms (Pss. 73-83). The names of these authors are supplied in the headings of the psalms. The authorship of some fifty psalms remains unknown. Because David wrote more of the psalms than anyone else and because he is known as "the sweet psalmist of Israel" (2 Sam. 23.1), the whole book is sometimes given the name, "The Psalms of David".

Groupings of Psalms

In addition to the five books within the Psalter, here are several other groupings of Psalms. One group is called the Pilgrimage Songs or the Songs of Ascent. These are Psalms 120 through 134. The pilgrimage psalms were sung by the Jews when they traveled to Jerusalem for the great feast days—the Day of Passover, the Day of Pentecost, and the Day of Atonement. Another group is called the Hallel, or Praise Psalms (Pss. 113-118, 146-150), and they were sung during certain festivals (The Hebrew word *hallel* means "praise"). For example, Psalms 113 through 118 were sung during the Feast of Tabernacles. Still another group of psalms are called the Elohim Psalms (or the Elohistic Psalter). This group gets its name from the Hebrew word *Elohim*, which is one of the Old Testament's names for God. In the Hebrew Bible there are several different names for God. *Elohim* is the general name that means "God", and the Hebrew word *Yahweh* is the personal name of Israel's God. Yahweh is usually translated "the Lord" or "Jehovah". In Psalms 1-41 and 84-150, the name "Yahweh" occurs much more often than the name "Elohim". However, Psalms 42-83 almost always use the word *Elohim* rather than *Yahweh*; therefore, those psalms are called the Elohistic Psalter.

Headings to the Psalms

Of the 150 psalms, 116 have headings (often called "superscriptions") containing one or more of the following: the author's name, the traditional setting of the psalm, typological designation, musical accompaniment, and other musical instructions. For example, the heading of the third Psalm reads, "A Psalm of David, when he fled from Absalom his son". Most scholars maintain that these headings are not a part of the original composition. However, the presence of the headings in both the Septuagint and in the Qumran scrolls suggests that they are very ancient. Furthermore, the fact that headings are found on the psalms that begin at 2 Samuel 23.1 and Habakkuk 3.1 may suggest that the practice of attaching a heading was a normal part of composition.

Different Types of Psalms

The book of Psalms is often characterized as a book of praises to the Lord. However, the very first psalm does not contain a single word of praise to God. We learn from the outset, therefore, that the book of Psalms contains songs of many different kinds. By employing a variety of psalm types, the Hebrew psalmists were able to respond in worship to the many different situations in their lives. Biblical scholars have identified five basic genres of psalms: the individual lament, the communal lament, the communal hymn, individual thanksgiving psalms, and royal psalms. Other scholars would also suggest categories such as wisdom psalms, psalms of Zion, historical psalms, and psalms of trust. These genres do not exhibit strict, ironclad structures, nor do they explain the nature of every song in the entire collection. Nevertheless, they are helpful guides to the basic forms of biblical psalmic expression.

Throughout this book we will say more about the psalms of lament, hymns, thanksgiving psalms, wisdom psalms, and psalms of trust. Other, less common types of psalms include the following:

Creation Psalms

The Creation Psalms focus on praising God as creator. For example, we read in Psalm 19, "The heavens declare the glory of God, and the firmament shows forth his handiwork" (v. 1). In Psalm 33 we are told, "By the word of the Lord the heavens were made, And all the host of them by the breath of His mouth" (v. 6). Psalm 24 declares, "The earth is the Lord's, and all its fullness, The world and those who dwell therein" (v. 1). A vital point of Old Testament teaching is that God created all things (see Gen. 1.1; Isa. 40.38). Other Songs of Creation include Psalms 8, 19, 65, 104, and 148.

Royal Psalms

The Royal Psalms are psalms that celebrate the rule of God's chosen Davidic king. They also praise God as eternal king. God is the king of Israel, the world, and the universe. He is Lord. The Royal Psalms include Psalms 2, 18, 20, 21, 45, 72, 101, 110, 132, and 144.

Historical Psalms

In the Historical Psalm the psalmist tells a portion of the history of Israel. Some of the historical psalms cover the story of Israel from the days of Abraham all the way up to the time when the psalm was written. Throughout these recitals of Israel's story, the psalms will praise God because he brought Israel out of Egypt and because he helped the patriarchs. These psalms, through their emphasis on God's faithfulness, provide encouragement to the Hebrew people. The Historical Psalms include Psalms 78 and 136.

The different kinds of Psalms teach us different aspects of worship. The presence of the Wisdom Psalms within Israel's song book suggests the importance of instruction as a part of worship. The Songs of Prayer demonstrate that biblical worship should provide a time and place for passionate prayer, for crying out to God. The Songs of Testimony demonstrate the value of telling our story to one another in the context of worship, praising God for specific acts of deliverance. The Hymns teach us to praise God for his unchangeable attributes. They show us that the goal of worship is absolute praise.

The Psalms Are Written in Poetic Form

Poetry may be defined as a verbal composition that intensively expresses feelings and ideas through its choice of exalted language and its patterned arrangement of words and phrases. This means that although poetry may appear in a variety of forms, it can be distinguished from ordinary writing by its use of (a) figurative language, (b) sound devices, (c) verse structure, and (d) emotive effect.

Poetic figurative language

One important feature of typical poetry is the use of figurative, symbolic language. Figurative language is the symbolic use of words to convey a meaning that is different from the literal meaning. The book of Psalms is filled with figurative language. The Psalmist declares, "The Lord is my shepherd" (Ps. 23.1). However, David is not literally a "sheep," and God is not literally a "shepherd". The symbol of the Lord as shepherd communicates that he is provider, guide and protector. Other examples of figurative language include the following:

"The Lord is my rock and my fortress" (2 Samuel 22.2)

"The Lord is my shepherd" (Ps. 23.1)

"But I am a worm, and no man" (Ps. 22.6)

"Their throat is an open tomb" (Ps. 5.9)

"He is a shield to all who trust in Him" (Ps. 18.30)

In Psalm 10, the psalmist uses a figure of speech to describe the wicked person: "He lies in wait secretly, as a lion in his den; He lies in wait to catch the poor" (Ps. 10.9). The words "like a lion" form a simile. The symbolism characterizes the wicked person as one who attacks those who are weaker, particularly the poor, and devours them for his own enjoyment.

The process for the purification of silver is used as symbolic language when the psalmist writes, "The words of the LORD are pure words, like silver tried in a furnace of earth, purified seven times" (Ps. 12.6). In order to remove any foreign elements, silver is melted and filtered. Silver that has been purified seven times is very, very pure. Similarly, the words of the Lord are very, very pure. There is nothing foreign or unclean in God's words.

An important figure of speech occurs in Psalm 51 when the psalmist repents to God and pleads to him, "Purge me with hyssop, and I shall be clean" (Ps. 51.7). Hyssop is a small bushy plant, an herb, which was used in the first passover and in Old Testament purification rituals. The hyssop was dipped into the blood of the sacrificial animal, and in the case of the passover, the blood was then spread upon the door. In the case of other ceremonies the blood was sprinkled upon the altar and the people (Exod. 24.6-8). Therefore, it is not the hyssop itself that purifies; it is the blood which is upon the hyssop that purifies. Thus, the hyssop is a metonymy for the blood.

We mentioned above that figures of speech add emphasis and get our attention. Sometimes this emphasis takes the form of an intentional and obvious exaggeration for the sake of making a point. For example, the psalmist describes the mariners on the sea when their ship rides the stormy waves: "They mount up to the heavens, They go down again to the depths" (Ps. 107.26). The words "heaven" and "depths" are symbols of the rise and fall of the gigantic waves as they lift the ship and then cause it to descend into the trough.

Because of his troubles, the psalmist often speaks of his grief and his weeping in exaggerated terms. His weeping is so profuse that he uses the symbolism of the "flood" and the "river". For example, he writes, "All night I make my bed swim; I drench my couch with my tears" (Ps. 6.6). Also, he says, "Rivers of water run down from my eyes, Because people do not keep your law" Ps. 119.136).

Because of its colorful and dramatic effect, the attributing of personal, human qualities to impersonal, nonhuman things is another important figure of speech that is used often in poetry. This type of figure is often used in scenes where God is being praised. For example, the psalmist declares, "Let the heavens rejoice, and let the earth be glad; Let the sea roar, and all its fullness" (Ps. 96.11). The heavens and the sea are not literally capable of glorifying God, but the psalmist calls upon them to rejoice and to be glad.

Finally, God is described with figurative language by attributing to him human form. As we know, God is a spirit (John 2:24) and does not possess a physical body. Describing the attributes of God can be difficult because God is a spirit; therefore, the biblical writers sometimes use human forms as a means of illustrating God's characteristics. For example, biblical poets use the word "hand" to signify the power of God. For example, David prays, "Save with your right hand, and hear me" (Ps. 108.6). The Psalms also make reference to God's "ears". David prays, "Bow down your ear to me, deliver me speedily" (Ps. 31.2). The words, "Bow down your ear to me", form a figure of speech through which David is asking for the Lord to hear his prayer. He is asking God to listen and to respond with the answer. In a similar fashion, the psalmist prays, "According to the greatness of your arm, preserve those who are appointed to die" (Ps. 79.11). The greatness of the Lord's "arm" represents his power and might. The Lord has the power to save us from death. In a few psalms, God is even described symbolically through reference to animal forms. For example, the psalmist speaks of God as if he has wings and feathers. He says, "He shall cover you with His feathers, And under His wings you shall take refuge" (Ps. 91.4). The wings of God represent his protective covering which he spreads over his people.

Poetic sound devices

In its sound, poetry exhibits intentional combinations of word sounds. Common poetic devices based upon sound include the repetition of consonant sounds at the beginning of words, such as the repetition of the letter "s" in the phrase, "the sweet smell of success". Another poetic sound device is the repetition of final consonant sounds, such as the repetition of the "st" sound in the saying, "First and last," the "ds" in "odds and ends," and the "t" in "short and sweet". Rhyme is the repetition of similar vowel-consonant combinations at the end of words; for example, "mention" rhymes with "attention" and "convention". Although rhyme is common in some poetry, it is uncommon in the Psalms. It is almost impossible to translate poetic sound devices from one language to another. In order to recognize poetic sounds in the Psalms, we must read from the original Hebrew text.

Poetic verse structure

Poetry normally utilizes verse structure that may include meter or rhythm. *The verse structure of Hebrew poetry is based upon parallelism of lines.* A poetic verse may consist of one, two, or three lines, but most often it will be two lines, with the second line related in some fashion to the first line. The second line may restate the thought of the first line; it may state the antithesis of the first line; or it may complete the thought of the first line.

Note the following examples:
The heavens declare the glory of God;
the skies proclaim the work of his hands (Ps. 19.1-2)
The second line repeats the same general idea using different terminology. "Heavens" and "skies" are synonyms, and "declare" and "proclaim" are synonyms. Another example is:
Do not fret because of evildoers,
Nor be envious of the workers of iniquity (Ps. 37.1)
In this case, "fret" is synonymous with "be envious," and "evildoers" is synonymous with "workers of iniquity,"

An example of the second line stating the antithesis of the first is:
The Lord knows the way of the righteous,
but the way of the ungodly shall perish (Ps. 1.6)
The second line states a truth that is the counterpart to the first line. In this instance, "the righteous" are opposite to "the ungodly"; and the actions of the Lord in the first line are opposite to his actions in the second line. Another example is:
For evildoers shall be cut off;
But those who wait on the Lord shall inherit the earth (Ps. 37.9)
Here we see that evildoers have a different end from those who wait upon the Lord.

There are still other kinds of connections between the first line and the second line of a Hebrew poetic verse. The second line may relate to the first line in the following ways:

The second line may provide the **reason** for the first line.

Blessed be the LORD!

because he has heard the voice of my supplications (Ps. 28.6)

The second line may ask a **question** based upon the first line.

For in death there is no remembrance of you;

in Sheol who can give you praise? (Ps. 6.5)

The second line my give the **answer** to the first line.

How can a young man keep his way pure?

By guarding it according to thy word (Ps. 119.9)

The second line may be a **quotation** that was introduced in the first line.

I had said in my alarm,

"I am driven far from your sight" (Ps. 31.22)

The first line may be something that is **"better"** than what is in the second line.

Better is a little that the righteous has

than the abundance of many wicked (Ps. 37.16)

The first line may be a **simile** with the meaning of the simile found in the second line.

As a father pities his children,

so the LORD pities those who fear him (Ps. 103.13)

Although parallelism of lines is the most distinctive mark of Hebrew poetry, another structural technique is the acrostic poem (e.g. Psalms 25, 34, 111, 112, 119, and 145). An acrostic is a poem in which each verse begins with successive letters of the Hebrew alphabet. Psalm 119 is unique in that it consists of 22 sections, one for each letter of the Hebrew alphabet, and every verse within a section begins with the same letter. Outside the book of Psalms, acrostics appear in Proverbs 31:10-31 and Lamentations Chapters 1, 2, and 4. In biblical times, the average believer did not possess a copy of the Scriptures. Therefore, it was important that people be able to memorize as much of the Bible as possible. Poetry was an aid to memorization, and acrostic poetry was even more easily remembered than standard poetry.

Poetic emotive effect

In its purpose, poetry intends not so much to inform the mind as to affect and move the heart. A significant attraction of biblical poetry is its ability to draw the reader into the poetic world through visual imagery, imaginative symbols, and appeals to the reader's emotions. This affective dimension of poetry speaks to the heart and to the passions with a fervent freshness and honesty.

Thus, the poetry of the Psalms gives witness to both the greatest joys of life and to its greatest agonies. For example, the emotions of the psalmist range from despair ("My heart is in anguish within me, the terrors of death have fallen upon me" Ps. 55.4) to elation ("Bless the Lord, O my soul: and all that is within me, bless his holy name" Ps. 103.1) and every feeling between those extremes.

Interpreting the Psalms

In order to interpret a psalm effectively we must give attention to its unique characteristics as poetry. That is, we must consider its (1) figurative language, (2) sound devices, (3) verse structure, and (4) emotive effect. In its content, poetry includes a high concentration of figurative language and word play. In its sound, poetry exhibits intentional combinations of word sounds. In its structure, biblical poetry utilizes verse structure that is based upon parallelism. In its effect, poetry intends not so much to inform the mind as to affect and move the heart.

The following process can be helpful in reading and interpreting the Psalms:

Outline the structure

What is the structure or the apparent divisions and subdivisions of the psalm? What distinguishes these parts? What holds them together? Is there a progression, development, climax, or focal point? Who is the speaker? To whom is the psalm addressed? Note the types of parallelism. Observe any movements between speakers, addressees, topics, and verb tenses. What type of psalm is this (wisdom, prayer, testimony, hymn)? What does that tell you about its purpose? Make a list of prominent themes and concepts that are repeated.

Examine the figures of speech and word play

Analyze the figures of speech. How do they impact the hearer and help to form the message? What are the prominent contrasts, comparisons, and symbolisms? How do they function in the passage? Can you identify any plays on words or sound devices? How do these devices impact your experience of the psalm?

Identify the affective mood

Poetry draws the reader into the poetic world through visual imagery, imaginative symbols, and appeals to the readers emotions. This affective dimension of poetry speaks to the heart and to the passions with a fervent freshness and honesty. What is the mood of the psalm? Is it joyful, hopeful, light, heavy, encouraging, convicting, mournful, sad, prayerful, thankful? Is there movement from one mood to another, such as from sadness to joy? How should we feel after studying this psalm? What parts of the psalm are particularly moving?

Observe contextual connections

How does the psalm reflect, respond, or relate to the surrounding psalms? To the book of Psalms as a whole? To the surrounding historical and sociological situations in ancient Israel and in the life of the psalmist? If the psalm has a superscription that suggests a context in the life of the psalmist, how does that context impact the meaning of the psalm? How does this psalm relate to the themes, patterns, and traditions found elsewhere in the Old Testament and in the ancient world?

Apply the psalm to your own life and church

The psalms emerge from Israel's life with God and express the struggles and joys of living in covenant with God. The psalms express our greatest fears, our deepest longings, and our fondest hopes. We may want to ask the following questions: What does this psalm teach us about God and how he relates to his people? What does it teach us about how we should relate to God and communicate with him? In light of our study, how is life informed, formed, or transformed by this psalm? What response is being called for? How might this passage be speaking beyond its own day even unto our own? How does this psalm inform us about our worship?

Experiencing the Psalms

It is hoped that this brief introduction to the Psalms will aid the reader in understanding the message that is found in these poignant prayers and powerful praises. The full richness of the Psalms can only be appreciated, however, when we move beyond analysis to experience. That is, the Psalms should not be seen as objects of study; rather, they should be seen as scenes of life. As we read a psalm, we should enter into its world, placing ourselves within its setting, its events, and its story. Let the words of the psalm be our words, expressing our thoughts, our feelings, and our relationship to God. Their inspiring use throughout the centuries has proven that the Psalms can serve as potent expressions of our prayers and our praises, our hopes and our dreams.

Chapter 1

The Heart of the Righteous

Psalm 1

¹ Blessed *is* the man
    Who walks not in the counsel of the ungodly,
    Nor stands in the path of sinners,
    Nor sits in the seat of the scornful;
² But his delight *is* in the law of the LORD,
    And in His law he meditates day and night.
³ He shall be like a tree Planted by the rivers of water,
    That brings forth its fruit in its season,
    Whose leaf also shall not wither;
    And whatever he does shall prosper.
⁴ The ungodly *are* not so,
    But *are* like the chaff which the wind drives away.
⁵ Therefore the ungodly shall not stand in the judgment,
    Nor sinners in the congregation of the righteous.
⁶ For the LORD knows the way of the righteous,
    But the way of the ungodly shall perish.

Happiness is a valued but illusive treasure. Yes, everyone wants to be happy and content. Everyone is chasing after happiness. But how do we achieve happiness? Where is happiness to be found? Does happiness come through material possessions? Does happiness come through personal success? Can we find happiness at the end of the rainbow? Is our happiness dependent upon our parents, our spouse, our children, our friends, or our boss?

According to Scripture, true happiness and genuine contentment occurs only within the context of our covenant relationship with God. We are created in the image of God and we are created to walk with god. We are "his people and the sheep of his pasture" (Ps. 100.3). He has created us to be his people, a people who will "show forth the praises of him who called us out of darkness and into his marvelous light" (1 Pet. 2.9).

We learn from Psalm 1 that real happiness is a matter of the heart. Psalm 1 is an introduction to the book of Psalms, and it was put at the very beginning of the Psalter to teach us that if we intend to serve God joyfully, we must serve him out of a heart that is attuned to his Word. The happy person, the true worshiper, finds "his delight" in the Word of God and in his Word he meditates day and night (Ps. 1.2). To delight in the Word of God is to have it in our hearts, to love it, to take pleasure in it, and to rejoice in it.

Therefore, if we intend to study the Psalms, to read the Psalms, to pray the Psalms, to sing the Psalms, and to experience the Psalms, we must first examine our hearts. If we are only interested in listening to the advice of wicked people, then we cannot hear what God would to say to us. If we walk on the pathway with sinners, then we will not be able to walk with Jesus. If we sit with scorners and boasters and those that rebel against God, we will not submit ourselves to the law of the Lord. So this is where we begin our study of the Psalms—with the heart of the believer.

The Blessedness of the Righteous

Psalm 1 encourages us to set our hearts on God and his word. This encouragement is framed in terms of a contrast between the blessedness of the righteous person and the ruination that comes to the wicked person. The Psalm can be divided into two parts:

The Blessedness of the Righteous (vv. 1-3)

The Ruination of the Wicked (vv. 4-6).

The righteous person is not influenced by evil and does not practice evil but instead delights in the Word of the Lord and meditates in it. The person who delights in the Word of God is like a flourishing and productive tree.

The wicked, in contrast to the righteous, are like worthless husks of grain. The wicked person has no standing at the place of judgment and no place in the congregation of the righteous. The Psalm's overall theme of the blessedness of the righteous (expressed through the contrast between the righteous and the wicked) is confirmed and sharpened in the final verse—"The Lord knows the way of the righteous, but the way of the wicked will perish". It is the Lord's providence that guarantees the blessedness of the righteous and the destruction of the wicked.

The Righteous are Favored by God

> Blessed is the man
> > Who walks not in the counsel of the ungodly,
> > Nor stands in the path of sinners,
> > Nor sits in the seat of the scornful; (Ps. 1:1)

Psalm 1 begins with words of affirmation: "Blessed is the man…" The word "blessed" is a translation of the Hebrew *asher*, which means "fortunate", "happy", or "favored". It refers to those who, because of their relationship to God and their walk with God, are living a blessed life. Psalm 1.1 carries an idea very similar to that of the beatitudes in Jesus' sermon on the mount: "Blessed are the poor in spirit … Blessed are those who mourn … Blessed are the meek …", and so forth (Mt. 5.3-11). In Ps. 1.1, however, the Hebrew word stands as an interjection, so we might translate it as, "Oh, the joys of the man" or "Oh, the happiness of the man". This happiness is a sense of well-being, of satisfaction, of being fortunate. Those who are blessed are flourishing, joyous, and satisfied with their lives. The translation "fortunate" captures the meaning to some degree, as long as we understand that good fortune is not accidental. The blessedness of Psalm 1 is not accidental; it is given by God to those who walk in his ways and who love his Word.

The following examples illustrate the meaning of the word "blessed" as found in Ps. 1.1:

- Blessed are your men and blessed are these your servants, who stand continually before you and hear your wisdom! (1 Ki. 10.8).
- Behold, blessed is the man whom God corrects (Job 5.17).
- Blessed are all those who put their trust in Him (Ps. 2.12).

- Blessed is he whose transgression is forgiven, Whose sin is covered (Ps. 32.1).
- Blessed is the man to whom the LORD does not impute iniquity, And in whose spirit there is no deceit (Psa 32.2).
- Blessed is the nation whose God is the LORD (Ps. 33.12 and 144.14)
- Blessed is the man who trusts in Him! (Ps. 34.8).
- Blessed is that man who makes the LORD his trust (Ps. 40.4 and Ps. 84.12)
- Blessed is he who considers the poor (Ps. 41.1).
- Blessed are those who dwell in Your house (Ps. 84.4).
- Blessed are those who keep justice, And he who does righteousness at all times! (Ps. 106.3).
- Blessed is the man who fears the LORD, Who delights greatly in His commandments (Ps. 112.1 and 128.1)
- Blessed is he who has the God of Jacob for his help, Whose hope is in the LORD his God (Ps. 146.5).
- Blessed is the man who finds wisdom, And the man who gains understanding (Prov. 3.13).
- The righteous man walks in his integrity; His children are blessed after him (Prov. 20.7).
- Blessed are all those who wait for [the Lord] (Isa. 30.18).

These verses help us to envision the deep and genuine happiness that accompanies those who seek after God and who give themselves in service to the needs of those around them.

The Righteous Follow the Right Path
Psalm 1 explains that in order to be truly happy and blessed we must not pursue evil. Again, verse 1 says,

> Blessed is the man
>> Who walks not in the counsel of the ungodly,
>> Nor stands in the path of sinners,
>> Nor sits in the seat of the scornful; (Ps. 1:1)

The "ungodly" are the "wicked",[1] those whose behavior is evil. Their words and deeds are contrary to God's character and also are hostile to those who are around them. The behavior of the wicked

---

[1] The Hebrew word *rasha* is better translated as "wicked'.

shows that they are not in a right relationship to God. The words "wicked" and "righteous" are used as opposites in the Bible.

According to Psalm 1.1, the righteous person avoids three kinds of evil. First, the righteous do not listen to wicked counsel: "Blessed is the man who does not walk in the counsel of the wicked". What does it mean to walk in the counsel of the wicked? Our walk is our behavior, and counsel is advice, plans, ideas, opinions, or values. If we are righteous, we do not model ourselves after those who are wicked. When we start looking for a model for advice and counsel, we must be sure that we listen to the right people instead of listening to the wicked. The wicked will not give us the kind of advice that we need to hear.

Second, the righteous do not accompany sinners in their activities. We read, "Blessed is the man who does not … stand in the path of sinners". A sinner is a person who is disobedient to God and is not obeying God's commandments. The path of sinners is their way of life, and to stand in their path is to become a part of their way of life.

Third, the righteous do not "sit in the seat of the scorners". A scorner is a person who is a scoffer, who boasts and rebels against God's authority. For us to sit in the seat of the scoffer is to remain there and make it a part of our surroundings. To sit there means that we acclimate to it, become a part of it, accommodate it, and assimilate the scornful attitude and way of life. Thus, the true worshipers are characterized in Ps. 1.1 first of all by what they do not do. They do not pursue evil; they are not interested in it, even though they may be tempted and tested.

I remember the sermon of a preacher who had turned to God at a later age—in his 30s. He had not been raised in church, and before his conversion he was an alcoholic. In his sermon he commented upon the paradox of sinning Christians. He said,

> I do not understand why Christians want to continue sinning. I lived in sin for 35 years, and it ruined my life. Why do people want to go after sin? I never got any good out of it. I do not want anything to do with it. I do not want it. I do not desire it.

He then told the story of the man who picked up a small snake when it was cold an immobile and put it in his coat. When the snake warmed up and was able to move, it bit him. Why did the snake bite the man? Because that is what snakes do. The old preacher understood that nothing good can come from our pursuing the ways of the wicked.

Sometimes we may see wicked people who appear to be prospering, and they seem to have it all together. Apparently, they have everything they need and want, but we can see only the outward appearance. God, however, knows what is in the heart. The wicked do not possess genuine and lasting joy. Material prosperity is fleeting and cannot bring happiness. Those who are righteous do not pursue evil, but instead the heart of the righteous person pursues the Word of God.

The Righteous Love the Word of God

After naming the evils that the righteous person avoids, the psalmist now turns to the positive attributes of the righteous. Blessed are those who do not pursue evil, but instead, their delight is in the law of the Lord. Verse 2 says,

> But his delight is in the law of the LORD,
> And in His law he meditates day and night.

In this verse, the word "law" does not mean a list of rules, regulations, orders, or commands. Instead, the Hebrew word for law is *torah*, which means instruction or teaching. The whole of God's word is his Torah, his teaching, his instruction. In the Hebrew tradition, the Pentateuch, which consists of the five books of Moses, is also called the Torah.

Psalm 1 introduces the book of Psalms as a book of teaching and instruction. It is God's torah (teaching) for us; and we should delight ourselves in it. Some Bible commentators have written that Psalm number one is all about obedience. They have said that a person must come to God in worship first as a duty or an obligation because it is something that God requires. However, the psalmist tells us that the righteous person *delights* in God's teaching. The righteous person loves God's teaching. The focus of Psalm 1.2 is not upon obligation or duty; instead, it's focus is upon the affections of the heart. The righteous person loves God's Word, takes pleasure in it, and meditates in it.

When we become a Christian, God changes our hearts. We are transformed by the power of the Gospel. The Apostle Paul writes, "Therefore, if anyone is in Christ, he is a new creation; old things have passed away; behold, all things have become new" (2 Cor.

5:17). When we become Christians our entire outlook changes, and our desires and affections are redirected. Instead of running *from* God, we run *to* God. Instead of avoiding the Word of God, we seek out the Word of God. Our hearts are attuned to God and to his Word. We are eager to spend time in prayer, and we long for deeper experiences of worship and praise.

Unfortunately, the initial joys of the Christian life are sometimes overshadowed by the passage of time and our love for God is eroded by disappointments, pain, and heartbreaks. Real worship happens when we go back and renew our first love. In the book of Revelation God tells the church at Ephesus, "You have lost your first love" (Rev. 2:4). We may be doing everything we are supposed to do—we may be going to church, we may be praying, we may even read the Bible—but if we are only doing these things out of duty and obligation then there is something missing. We should have a desire, a passion in our hearts. We might compare our relationship to God with that of our spouse. Married people fall out of love because they forget why they love the person that they married, and they forget how to love that person. Their hearts begin to wander, and they forget about the person they love. Part of the importance of maintaining a good marriage is to always maintain a sense of delight in the spouse. Married people must maintain a desire to be with their partner. If that desire is lost, it must be regained or else the marriage will fail. Those who enjoy a long and happy marriage have learned how to nurture the love and delight for their spouse.

The righteous person delights in the Torah, the Law of the Lord. The word "delight" has reference to the affections. It is defined as " to take joy in," "to take pleasure in." It denotes the direction of one's heart or passion," a pleasurable emotional attraction. Outside the Psalter, "delight" can denote the attraction between a man and a woman—we read that the son of Hamor "delighted in Jacob's daughter" (Gen 34:19). Also, "delight" can refer to God's pleasure in his people and their actions—the Israelites are hopeful that Yahweh "delights" in them (Num 14:8), and Samuel insinuates that Yahweh has greater "delight" in Saul's obedience than in his sacrifices (1 Sam 15:22). The Lord takes pleasure in his people. He delights in saving the sinner; there is rejoicing in heaven when a person is converted (Luke 15:7). We are his people, and he delights to see us grow, he delights to see us worship, and he delights to hear us pray. He is sitting on his throne at all times with his ear tuned to earth, delighting in the words, in the songs, and in the praises of God's people. God delights in us, and we delight in him.

Psalm 1 suggests the need for obedience, but it is an obedience that is generated by love and that springs from a transformed life. Obedience that is based upon legalism leads only to frustration. Obedience must flow out of our love for God. That is why Jesus said that the greatest commandment is that we love God wholeheartedly. If we love God with all our hearts, then it is not a burden to obey him and to do what he asks.

In light of the Scriptures mentioned above, "delight" should be understood as an affective term, and its prominence in Psalm 1 testifies to the importance of the affections in the life of the righteous. Psalm 1:2, however, is not alone in its affirmation that the righteous are those who take "delight" in the Torah of Yahweh. A similar sentiment is echoed four times in Psalm 119 (vv. 70, 77, 92, and 174). Furthermore, the Psalter calls for not only a delight in the "Torah" but also a delight in the Lord's "statutes" (119:16), his "testimonies" (119:24), and his "commandments" (112:1; 119:47).

The delight of the believer in the Lord and in his Word is expressed in the following scriptures:

Psalm 37:4 "Delight yourself also in the LORD, And He shall give you the desires of your heart."

Psalm 40:8 "I delight to do Your will, O my God, And Your law is within my heart."

Psalm 119:16 "I will delight myself in Your statutes; I will not forget Your word."

Psalm 119:24 "Your testimonies also are my delight And my counselors."

Psalm 119:35 "Make me walk in the path of Your commandments, For I delight in it."

Psalm 119:47 "And I will delight myself in Your commandments, Which I love."

Psalm 119:70 "... I delight in Your law."

Psalm 119:77 "… Your law is my delight."

Psalm 119:174 "I long for Your salvation, O LORD, And Your law is my delight."

Psalm 19:9-10 "… the judgments of the LORD … More to be desired are they than gold, yea, than much fine gold: sweeter also than honey and the honeycomb."

Psalm 119:14 "I have rejoiced in the way of thy testimonies, as much as in all riches."

Psalm 119:32 "I will run toward your commandments."

Psalm 119:40 "Behold, I have longed after thy precepts."

Psalm 119:54 "Thy statutes have been my songs."

Psalm 119:72 "The law of thy mouth is better unto me than thousands of gold and silver."

Psalm 119:97 "O how love I thy law! it is my meditation all the day."

Psalm 119:103 "How sweet are thy words unto my taste! yea, sweeter than honey to my mouth!"

Psalm 119:111 "Thy testimonies have I taken as an heritage for ever: for they are the rejoicing of my heart."

Psalm 119:113 "… thy law do I love."

Psalm 119:127 "Therefore I love thy commandments above gold; yea, above fine gold."

Psalm 119:129 "… wonderful are your testimonies."

Psalm 119:131 "I opened my mouth and panted, For I longed for Your commandments."

Psalm 119:140 "Your word is very pure; Therefore Your servant loves it."

Psalm 119:143 "Trouble and anguish have overtaken me, Yet Your commandments are my delights."

Psalm 119:162 "I rejoice at Your word As one who finds great treasure."

Affection for the Law, which Psalm 1 evokes, is consistent with the teaching of other psalms, and the word "delight" is not the only term that suggests the importance of affection for the Law. The writer of Psalm 119 declares, "Oh, how I love your Law! It is my contemplation all the day" (v. 97, cf. vv. 113, 127, 140, 163, and 165). Psalm 19 praises God's "law," "testimony," "precepts," "commandments," and "judgments," saying, "They are more desirable than gold, yes, than much fine gold: sweeter also than honey and the honeycomb" (v. 10, cf. Ps. 119:72, 103). Through the use of other affective terms the hearer of the Psalms is encouraged to put the Torah "in his heart" (37:31; 40:8), to "rejoice" in the Torah (119:14, 111, 162), to "long for" Yahweh's precepts (119:40), to "rejoice" in his statutes (19:8), to "desire" his commandments (119:131), to "run" toward them (119:32), and make them his "songs" (119:54) and his "desire". The hearer is enjoined to "rejoice" and "be glad" because of Yahweh's judgments (48:11; 97:8). The Psalmist pleads longingly, "Open my eyes, that I may see wondrous things out of your Torah" (119:18, cf. v. 129). The tenor of the Psalms is similar to that of Jeremiah who exclaims, "Your word was for me the joy and rejoicing of my heart" (Jer 15:16).

The above texts demonstrate a common interest in the affective dimension of Torah devotion. To delight in the Torah is an affective inclination, a passionate disposition. To delight in the Torah is to rejoice in it, to love it, to long for it, to desire it more than gold, and to enjoy it more than honey. The words of the Torah, penetrate the heart, stir the emotions, warn the intellect, and energise the will. The emphasis of Psalm 1 is not upon deeds but delight, not on duty but desire, not on obedience but on affections that are rightly oriented towards God. Psalm 1 points to the inner life of the heart that longs to hear God's voice and that welcomes God's Word with affection and joy. If we delight in the Word of God, we will read it, study it, search it, and allow it to speak into our lives.

The Righteous Meditate in the Word of God

The righteous person delights in the Torah, and that delight is manifested through continual reflection upon it. The meaning of the Hebrew word *hagah*, translated here as "meditate," is not entirely clear. What is clear, however, is that it does not correspond exactly to the English "meditate," which means "to exercise the mind in thought or reflection."[2] While "meditate" often denotes a silent activity, the Hebrew *hagah* seems in most cases to signify some sort of audible, vocal utterance. It has been defined as "moan, growl, utter, speak, muse," and "utter, mutter, moan (mourn, KJV), meditate, devise, plot."

Observe how the word "meditate" (*hagah*) is used in the following Scriptures:

"This book of the Torah shall not depart out of your mouth; you shall meditate in it day and night" (Josh. 1:8).

"My mouth will praise you with joyful lips. When I remember you on my bed, I meditate on you in the night watches" (Ps. 63:5b-6).

"I remember my song in the night ... I will meditate on all your work, and muse on your mighty deeds" (Ps. 77:6-12).

"I remember the days of old; I meditate on all your works; I muse on the work of your hands" (Ps. 143:5).

In light of the fact that the Torah is to be in Joshua's "mouth," it seems likely that his meditation would include some form of utterance. Also, two of the three examples from Psalms include parallels to the word "muse" (Ps. 77:12 and 143:5), which may signify "rehearsing" a matter and most often includes speech (Ps. 55:2, 18; 64:2; 69:13; 102:1; 105:2; 142:3). Furthermore, the context of singing is evident in Psalms 63 and 77, which suggests that in these texts meditation is expressed in a song of praise.

In the Hebrew, therefore, meditation likely denotes a thoughtful, deliberate utterance, which is spoken softly or even unintelligibly. Meditation on the Torah might be accomplished through the reading of the written text, as in the case of Josh. 1:8. Or for those who do not have access to the written Torah, meditation could be in the form of recitation from memory or of rehearsing the traditional narratives. Meditation might also signify the murmuring of one whose thoughts are occupied in deep reflection upon God's words and deeds. To meditate means to lose oneself in God's Word and to be filled with thoughts of God's deeds or his will. In Ps. 1:2, the word "meditate" is an expression of innermost delight in the Word of God.

---

[2] John Simpson & Edmund Weiner, eds., *Oxford English Dictionary* (Oxford: Oxford University Press, 2nd Ed., 1989).

As shown in the Scriptures above, meditation can signify the utterance of a song; therefore, the meditation of Ps. 1:2 can include singing of Psalms as one of its modes of expression. Another connection between meditation and singing is the word *higgaion*, which signifies a Psalm of meditation (see Pss. 9:16 and 92:3). Still another connection between Torah and song, is that when Moses wrote the book of the Law, he also wrote a commemorative song (Deut. 31:22-24). The song is taught to the people, and the book of the law is handed over to the Levites and elders. Thus, Deut. 31–32 identifies law-contemplation with worshipful song-singing. It is the song which will be forever known by the people (Deut 31:21). Therefore, modes of meditation include reading the Torah, reciting Scripture, and reflecting on the Word. Yet worshipful singing of psalms may be the form of meditation that is most appropriate to the context of Ps. 1:2.

Finally, it should not be overlooked that the commendation to meditate in the Torah appears within a Psalm, suggesting perhaps that Psalm 1 itself becomes a demonstration of what is envisioned in 1:2. Therefore, as an introduction to the Psalter, Ps. 1:2 may conceive of the Psalms as passionate meditations on the Torah. The content of the Psalter could certainly support such a conclusion since numerous explicit references and allusions to elements of the Torah are found throughout the Psalms. For example, Ps. 19:1-6 is a delight-filled meditation on the Torah's claim that God is creator: "The heavens declare the glory of God, and the firmament shows his handiwork" (v. 1). Psalm 44:1-3 is a passionate meditation on the conquest story: "You drove out the nations with your hand" (v. 2a). The psalms of prayer often appeal to the justice that is demanded by the Torah. Psalm 78 delights in Yahweh's mercy from the time of Jacob to David. Psalm 105 meditates on the Abrahamic covenant (vv. 9-22) and delights in the salvation of the exodus (23-45). Perhaps the singing of the Psalms is not the only way of taking delight in the Torah, but it is one way. It follows that the promise of "blessedness" (Ps. 1:1) accrues to the person who reads, recites, and sings the Psalms with delight.

If we delight in the Word of God we will spend much time absorbing its message. The Psalmist declare that the righteous person delights in the Law of the Lord "and in his law he meditates day and night" (Ps. 1:2). The believer should be continually occupied with thoughts of God and his Word. Meditation on the Law of the Lord requires a commitment of time. Modern readers often try to read through the Bible hurriedly, but this is a mistake. Reading the Bible is not improved by speed; there is no benefit to being in a hurry. In fact, you are a lot better off if you can find a place where you can read it out loud and slow down so that it can sink in and you can think about it and meditate on it. When you read the Bible, you should not hurry through it. You should slow down and meditate on it. You should read it and repeat it because you are trying to get a firm grip on God's word.

The Jews even have the practice of not only reading the Scripture but also reading prayer books and other inspirational books. They have a kind of movement where they rock back and forth as they read. This is their tradition; it started in biblical times with the idea of meditating. It goes back at least as far as Joshua 1.8. He says, "This book of the Law shall not depart from your mouth, but you shall meditate in it day and night". It is in his mouth; he is saying it while he is meditating on it. "And you may observe to do according to all that is written in it". So he is saying it, he is meditating on it, and he is doing it.

The Righteous Flourish like a Fruitful Tree

> He shall be like a tree planted by the rivers of water,
>> That brings forth its fruit in its season,
>> Whose leaf also shall not wither;
>> And whatever he does shall prosper. (Ps. 1:3)

By meditating on God's Word, getting into it, reading it, going over it, and studying it, God will speak to you. Those who delight in the Law of the Lord and meditate in it will be like a flourishing tree. The person who does not do the evil but delights in and meditates in God's word is like a tree planted by the rivers of water, bringing forth fruit in its season. His leaf does not wither, and whatsoever he does shall prosper. This is the blessedness of giving your heart and mind to God's word. If you are in the word of God, reading it, studying it, meditating on it, and obeying it, then God will direct your steps and you will be like a tree planted by the rivers of water.

The tree that is "planted" by the rivers of waters is not a tree that springs up spontaneously, but one that is set out in a favorable place, and that is cultivated with care. The word "rivers" does not here quite express the sense of the original Hebrew. The Hebrew word *peleg* refers to irrigation channels, canals, trenches. The allusion is to the method of irrigating lands by making artificial channels to convey the water from a larger stream, or from a lake. In this way, the water was distributed in all directions. The whole land of Egypt was irrigated in this manner, and it was in this way that its extraordinary fertility was secured. The rivers of water are the irrigation channels, and the trees are planted there because it is a well-watered place. It is not an accidental thing; it is a planted tree. God plants us where we need to be, where we can prosper.

The righteous person is like a tree that brings forth fruit in season. The idea is that of a tree which, at the proper season of the year, is loaded with fruit. The image is one of great beauty. The fruit is not untimely. It does not ripen and fall too soon, or fall before it is mature; and the crop is abundant.

Furthermore, his leaves do not wither. The leaves are unaffected by the heat of the sun and the drying effects of the hot winds. Like a tree that is green and flourishing, the person who delights in God's Word will be protected from every danger that comes their way.

Finally, "whatsoever he does will prosper". This tree is always healthy; it is extending its roots, circulating its sap, putting forth fruitbuds, blossoms, leaves, or fruit; all in their proper seasons. So the righteous person is ever taking deeper root growing stronger in grace and increasing in the Holy Spirit. Much fruit to the glory and praise of God is continually produced.

If we desire to obtain permanent prosperity and happiness, it is to be found only by pursuing God and his Word. Jesus tells us, "Seek first the kingdom of God and his righteousness and all these things will be added to you" (Matt. 6:33). Of course we understand that we may sometimes face times of trouble and tribulation. Even the righteous are subject to the calamities that come upon a people in times of commercial distress, in seasons of war, of famine, and pestilence. But still, a holy life will be followed by God's blessing, and the righteous will "rejoice in the Lord always" (Phil. 4:4). It is this great and important truth which it is the primary message of Psalm 1.

The Ruination of the Wicked (vv. 4-6)

> The ungodly are not so,
>> But are like the chaff which the wind drives away. (Ps. 1:4-6)

The Wicked Live Worthless Lives

Unlike the righteous, the wicked person does not flourish and has no status among God's people. The wicked are not like a fruitful tree; instead, they are "like the chaff which the wind drives away." The wicked are like the chaff (also called "husk") that is separated from the grain. The ancient process called "winnowing" is in view here. After the farmers harvested the grain, they would beat it with a stick or have a cow trample it thoroughly. The beating and trampling would separate the grain from the husk. Then the farmer would throw the grain up in the air, and the wind would blow away the husk. If there was no wind at the time, the farmer would blow the husk away with a large fan. The husk that the wind blows away is worthless.

The wicked are not like a tree in any respect. They are not even like a decaying tree, a barren tree, a dead tree, for either of these would suggest some idea of stability or permanency. They may have their mansions, but those mansions will crumble. They may have their riches, but those riches will not endure. They may have their lands, but in the end, they will lose those lands because "the meek shall inherit the earth" (Ps. 37:11). They are like dry and worthless chaff driven off by the wind. They are of no value at all; they are intrinsicly worthlessness. They are worthless to both God and to their fellow humans. In spite of their boasting, their riches, and their high positions, they are worthless in regard to all the purposes for which God made them.

The idea of the wicked being like chaff is picked up in the Gospel of Matthew, where John the Baptist proclaims, "His winnowing fan is in His hand, and He will thoroughly clean out His threshing floor, and gather His wheat into the barn; but He will burn up the chaff with unquenchable fire" (Matt. 3:12). John's prophecy leads us to consider the next verse of Psalm 1.

The Wicked Are Without Standing

Therefore the ungodly shall not stand in the judgment,
>> Nor sinners in the congregation of the righteous. (Ps. 1:5)

In verse 5, we learn first that the wicked have no standing in the judgment. The idea seems to be derived from the act of standing up to be tried, or to receive a sentence. But when they come to be judged, they will have nothing to plead in their behalf. Therefore, they will be condemned, and they will be unable to remain standing. Their knees will buckle from terror and dread of the sentence of guilt. In Rev. 6:17, John speaks of the days of great tribulation, and he says, "For the great day of His wrath has come, and who is able to stand?"

We also learn in verse 5 that the sinners have no place in the congregation of the righteous. The sinners are not reckoned or regarded as belonging to the righteous. In all the places where the righteous are assembled, the sinners will have no place. Where God's people assemble to worship God, the sinners have no place. Where the righteous stand in God's presence to glorify his holy name, the sinners have no place. Where the righteous gather in heaven and are gathered together to receive their reward, the sinner has no place. The sinner has no place in the congregation of the people of God.

The righteous long for heaven, for no evil will dwell there. On earth, the Church is impure--the tares grow in the same field as the wheat (Matt. 13:25-40). Like Lot, whose righteous soul was tormented by the sinful deeds of the people of Sodom (2 Pet. 2:8), we are continually distressed by the sinfulness of our generation. But there will be no sin in heaven. We are told in Rev. 21:8, "But the cowardly, unbelieving, abominable, murderers, sexually immoral, sorcerers, idolaters, and all liars shall have their part in the lake which burns with fire and brimstone, which is the second death." Sinners have no place in the assembly of the righteous.

Having no place, it follows that they have no authority or power there. The tyrants of the world are powerless and helpless in the assembly of the saints. Abusers of the weak will face judgment at the hands of the Almighty avenger, who is the father of the orphan and husband to the widow. Even now there exist two worlds, the kingdom of this world and the kingdom of God. In large part the sinners rule this world, but in the kingdom of God, sinners should have no influence. The Church stands as a beacon of light in this darkness and as a refuge for those who have suffered at the hands of Satan and his servants.

The Wicked Are Wiped Out in the End

> For the LORD knows the way of the righteous,
>> But the way of the ungodly shall perish. (Ps. 1:6)

There is a reason that the righteous are like a flourishing tree. There is a reason that the wicked are like worthless chaff and that they cannot stand in the judgment. All of these truths are based upon one foundation—"the Lord knows." In the book of Exodus, the Israelites were slaves in Egypt and they were struggling and made to serve the Egyptians. They cried out to God because of their task-masters and because of the hard bondage. But the Lord heard their groaning and their sighs because of their taskmasters. We read that "the Lord knew" (Exod. 2:25). The Psalmist declares that the Lord knows the way of the righteous, whether it is good or whether it is bad. The Lord knows, he sees, and he hears. Though we walk through the valley of the shadow of death, the Lord knows our way and guides us with his staff. He numbers the hairs of our heads and he will no allow us to fall. Job said, "He knows the way that I take; when he has tried me, I shall come forth as gold" (Job 23:10).

The Lord knows our pathway, but the way of the wicked is for destruction. "Perish" means to be destroyed, to be wiped out. It may not be immediate destruction. You will find that later on in Psalm 73, for example, where the psalmist complains that the wicked are prospering. He says, "But then I went to the house of God and I learned of their end." Their end is destruction. Their projects, designs and operations, will perish. And in the day of judgment they shall be condemned to the everlasting lake of fire. "As wax melts before fire, so the wicked shall perish before the presence of God" (Ps. 68:2).

Conclusion

Many significant lessons can be learned from the study of Psalm 1. Let us review what we have studied and reflect on the implications of this Psalm.

Psalm 1 Emphasizes the Value of Teaching

The first Psalm contains no prayer, and it contains no praise. It is a teaching psalm, a Psalm of Instruction. Psalms of Instruction are songs that help us to draw closer to God through their teachings. Some people call these the Wisdom Psalms because many of the topics in these psalms are also found in the wisdom books of Proverbs, Ecclesiastes, and Job. These characteristic themes are the family, God's law, justice, life's choices, life's inconsistencies, the trust or fear of God, and the contrast between the wicked person and the righteous person. The following chart shows the presence of these themes in Psalms 1, 73, and 128:

	Ps. 1	Ps. 73	Ps. 128
The wicked and the righteous	1-3, 4-6		
God's retribution	3, 6	18, 19, 27	2, 5
God's law	2		
Trust/fear of God		21-24	1, 4
Inconsistencies of life		1-20	
Family			3, 6

Other psalms of instruction are Psalms 32, 37, 49, 78, 112, 119, 127, 133, and 145.

The presence of these wisdom psalms within Israel's song book suggests the importance of instruction as a part of worship. Some churches today have abandoned Christian education. They have eliminated Sunday School and other education classes. However, the biblical example of worship includes the teaching component. The book of Psalms begins with teaching and includes teaching throughout the book. We will learn in other psalms that prayer and praise are valuable aspects of worship, but the very first psalm emphasizes worship as a learning experience, and the curriculum for learning is the "law of the Lord" (Ps. 1.2). We read in the New Testament that when the early Christians gathered together for worship they combined teaching, fellowship, eating, praying, and praise:

> they continued steadfastly in the teaching of the apostles and in fellowship, in the breaking of bread, and in prayers ... with one accord in the temple, and breaking bread from house to house ... praising God (Acts 2.42-47).

Psalm 1 Invites Us to Hear God's Word

Psalm 1 pronounces the Lord's approval of and blessings upon those who are righteous. The righteous are identified by their resistance to the lure of wicked counsel and by their affection for the "law of the Lord." The psalm points to the affections rather than to behavior as the key element of the righteous person—"his delight is in the Torah of the Lord and in his Torah he meditates day and night" (Ps. 1.2). Instead of demanding legalistic obedience to the Law, Psalm 1 evokes affection for the Law. The blessed ones are thus identified by the attitude of their hearts—their love for God's Word. Psalm 1.2 teaches us that delight in the torah is the determining and effective disposition of the truly happy life.

In its role as an introduction to the Psalter, Psalm 1 sets the tone for encountering the Psalms, identifying the attitude that is necessary to enter the Psalter. Psalm 1 suggests that right worship begins with rightly oriented affections. When Psalm 1 invites meditation on the torah as a response to God's self-revelation, it becomes its own example. It offers itself as a model of torah meditation, a model which is picked up and expanded by the psalms that follow. The Psalms, therefore, serve as exemplars of what it means to delight in the torah of the Lord.

This affective approach to the Psalms is evident in the writings of Martin Luther, whose comments on Ps. 1.2 show his own passionate affection for the Law of the Lord:

> [This affection] is the pure desire of the heart … it is not only the love of the Law but also a loving delight in the Law which the world and the prince of the world can destroy and defeat neither by prosperity nor by adversity. Yet through need, ignominy, the cross, death, and hell this "desire" breaks through to victory.[3]

Psalm 1 Guarantees Happiness to the Righteous

Our lives are filled with uncertainties, and our children are faced with competing viewpoints on how they should live their lives. They see the lifestyles of the wealthy and the behavior of sports heroes and movie stars, and they question the value of serving God in this world. Is there really joy in living for Jesus, or can we find an equal amount of joy in serving ourselves? Are the poor in spirit really blessed, or is it the proud and arrogant who find prosperity? Are those who hunger and thirst for righteousness really filled, or

---

[3] Pelikan *et al.* (eds.), *Luther's Works*, XIV, p. 295.

should they instead settle for the "lust of the flesh, the lust of the eyes, and the pride of life" (1 John 2:16)? Does the universe operate according to dependable laws in which good is rewarded and evil is punished? Does God really care? If so, is he involved in the outcomes of our decisions?

Psalm 1 assures us that God honors our faithfulness, that evil will be punished and good will be rewarded. In spite of the apparent randomness in the universe, Psalm 1 guarantees that God's Law governs the destiny of us all. God cares for his people, and God acts on their behalf. Yes, there is joy in serving the Lord—"joy unspeakable and full of glory" (1 Pet. 1:8). Yes, God knows who we are and where we live. It is God's providence that guarantees the blessedness of the righteous and the destruction of the wicked.

❧ Chapter 2 ❧

Touching God through Urgent Prayer

Psalm 13
To the Chief Musician. A Psalm of David.

¹ How long, O LORD? Will You forget me forever?
　　How long will You hide Your face from me?
² How long shall I take counsel in my soul,
　　Having sorrow in my heart daily?
　　How long will my enemy be exalted over me?
³ Consider *and* hear me, O LORD my God;
　　Enlighten my eyes, Lest I sleep the *sleep of* death;
⁴ Lest my enemy say, "I have prevailed against him";
　　Lest those who trouble me rejoice when I am moved.
⁵ But I have trusted in Your mercy;
　　My heart shall rejoice in Your salvation.
⁶ I will sing to the LORD,
　　Because He has dealt bountifully with me.

I was awakened early one morning by the ringing of the telephone. As a pastor, I knew that a phone call that early in the morning usually indicated either an emergency or a tragedy. The caller was my brother-in-law Stan Rankin, and he confirmed that a tragedy had indeed occurred. Charlie Stott, one of our close friends from college had committed suicide. This news came as a terrible shock, and I was filled with disbelief. In college, Charlie had been a spiritual giant in my eyes. His level of devotion to God, the depth of his prayers, the genuineness of his faith, his willingness to sacrifice and bear the cross, his passion to win the lost, and his exuberant generosity were evident to all who knew him. Having been a close friend of Charlie, I found it difficult to comprehend how he could have lost hope to the extent that he would take his own life.

I learned later that Charlie had gotten caught up in the prosperity gospel. He had come to believe that those who are righteous will always be blessed with spiritual and material prosperity. He had come to believe that the righteous are always victorious and that by faith they will quickly defeat all opposition that comes their way. But Charlie's expectation of prosperity had not been realized, and he had not achieved a worry-free life. According to the prosperity gospel, believers can live in perfect health—sickness is a result of unbelief. Charlie, however, had not been able to reach the level of faith that is required to live in perfect health and in continual victory. Consequently, he was unable to come to grips with the inconsistencies that developed between his idea of prosperity and the realities that he faced. Charlie could not bear the thought that his faith was insufficient. His despair grew so intense that it drove him to suicide.

Suffering is a Part of Life

What Charlie needed to know was that the prosperity gospel is insufficient—it is an incomplete Gospel. It focuses upon only one side of the biblical picture of faith. And he also needed to understand that his struggles were nothing new—the ancient Israelites faced similar theological tensions. We learned in Psalm 1 that the righteous are blessed and the wicked are punished. The Lord knows the way of the righteous, and he insures that they are prosperous. They are like a flourishing tree whose leaves do not wither and whose fruit is abundant. Psalm 1 presents a world that operates according to divinely established rules and principles. It suggests a theology in which justice prevails in the world—the righteous are blessed and the wicked are punished.

The worldview of Psalm 1 is affirmed in Psalm 2 where the blessings of righteousness are extended to rulers and to nations. We learn that the "nations rage ... against the Lord and against his anointed" (Psalm 2:1-2), and these rebellious nations are broken and destroyed by the power of God (v. 9). But the people who "serve the Lord with fear" can rejoice because "Blessed are all those who put their trust in him" (vv. 11-12).

However, if we stop reading after Psalm 2, our theology will be incomplete. Psalm 3 presents the other side of the biblical picture of faith in which the neat, tidy, well-ordered theology of Psalms 1 and 2 gives way to a theology that allows for the realities of life, realities that include struggle, injustice, abuse, doubt, fear, and the testing of our faith.

As soon as we hear in Psalms 1 and 2 that God blesses the righteous and that God blesses the nations that obey him, we run up against these words in Psalm 3:

> [1] Oh Lord, those who trouble me are increased.
>   Many are they who rise up against me.
> [2] Many are saying to me,
>   "There is no help for you in God"".

In Psalm 3 the Psalmist is challenged and tested, and his faith is put on trial. Likewise, in Psalm 13:1-2, we hear David pray,

> [1] How long, O Lord? Will You forget me forever?
>   How long will You hide Your face from me?
> [2] How long shall I take counsel in my soul,
>   Having sorrow in my heart daily?
>   How long will my enemy be exalted over me?

Psalms 3 and 13 teach us that the righteous will face suffering, trials, and tests. These prayer psalms reflect the experience of righteous Job. The Bible declares that Job was "perfect and upright; he feared God and shunned evil" (Job 1:1). Satan appeared before God and accused Job of being a "fair weather" believer. Satan said to God, "You put a hedge of protection around him. If you take away the hedge, Job will curse you to your face". God had confidence in Job's faith and replied to Satan, "I will remove my protection over Job and you may attack him in whatever way you like, only do not take his life". Consequently, Job's faith was tested. Job, however, did not understand what was happening to him; he did not know what was going on. All he knew was that his children were killed, his property was destroyed, his houses were knocked down, his cattle and his sheep were all stolen, his body is sick from head to toe, he is sitting on an ash heap, and he is asking God to just let him die because he is in misery.

The theology of Psalms 1 and 2 is important as a foundation to our relationship with God. It is vital that we are able to trust in God's goodness, sovereignty, and providence. We must also understand, however, that our faith in God will be tested—yes, our faith *must* be tested. The righteousness of Job resulted in prosperity, but then Job's faith was tested through suffering. Job's suffering did not come to him because of his weakness or failure but because of his strength of character and his trust in the Lord. Jesus promises, "In the world you shall have tribulation" (John 16:33), and Paul declares, "Those who live godly in Christ Jesus will suffer persecution" (2 Timothy 3:12). To those who suffer, Peter writes, "Beloved, do not think it strange concerning the fiery trial which is to try you, as though some strange thing happened to you" (1 Peter 4:12). Testings, trials, hardships, and sufferings are not a sign that we have failed, rather they are a normal part of the Christian life, and their purpose is to make us stronger.

Some would say that we ought to live in Psalm 1, and that when suffering comes our way, we only need to speak a positive confession and ignore our problem, and it will go away. But Psalm 3, Psalm 13, and other scriptures would tell us that life is not so simple. There are days when our rejoicing turns to mourning and God's blessing upon our life is in doubt. Our lives are turned upside down because tragedy, trouble, upheaval, chaos, confusion, and uncertainty come our way. We do not know why it comes or how it happens. When Jesus' disciples heard that Pilate had killed a number of Galilean Jews and mixed their blood with the sacrifices, they questioned Jesus how this sort of thing could happen to God's people. Jesus explained to his disciples that righteous people sometimes suffer:

> And Jesus answered and said to them, "Do you suppose that these Galileans were worse sinners than all other Galileans, because they suffered such things? I tell you, no ... Or those eighteen on whom the tower in Siloam fell and killed them, do you think that they were worse sinners than all other men who dwelt in Jerusalem? I tell you, no ... (Luke 13:2-5).

Jesus did not offer a reason why the Galilean Jews were made to suffer and he did not explain why the tower fell on the people of Siloam. But he did insist that their suffering was not on account of their sin or disobedience. Jesus taught us that suffering is a part of living in this world. Until the kingdom of God is fully realized, Christians will face tests and trials.

On January 12, 2010, a 7.0 magnitude earthquake struck Haiti and devastated the capital city, Port-au-Prince. It has been estimated that 316,000 people were killed. The Presidential palace, Parliament and many other important structures were destroyed, along with countless homes and businesses, leaving many homeless. The massive earthquake destroyed not only the homes of sinners but also the homes of Christians. Not only were government buildings and corporate offices leveled but also Churches were flattened. Yes, the wicked suffered greatly, but so did the righteous. There are perhaps two or three million Christians in Haiti—Church of God, Assemblies of God, Baptist, Methodist, and other denominations—for whom this earthquake was a grim test of faith.

How should good people react to tragedy? How do we make sense of the suffering that comes our way? As we watched the television, we saw the pain, the suffering, and the death of believers in Haiti. We should not say to them, "If you will just believe God and confess your faith, you will feel better and all will be well". When a mother is pulling her lifeless infant out from under the rubble, there is nothing we can say to make her feel good. It hurts; it really hurts. In this chapter, we will study Psalm 13, and we will learn how to respond to experiences of pain and testing. When we are really hurting, we need to be able to take our hurts to God in prayer.

The Psalms of Prayer

In the book of Psalms, these times of hurting produce the Psalms of Prayer. The Psalms of Prayer are urgent prayers that may be motivated by several categories of need. They may be prayers for overcoming the enemy, prayers for healing, or prayers of repentance because of sin. For example, in Psalm 51 David prays, "Wash me thoroughly from my iniquity, and cleanse me from my sin" (v. 2). These different kinds of prayers have a similar form that Bible scholars call the "lament" or "lamentation". The lament (what I have called the Psalm of Prayer) is the most common type of Psalm in the Bible. You probably have observed that one entire book of the Bible is made up of lament and carries the name "Lamentations".

Psalm 13

Psalm 13 is a lament, an urgent prayer. It follows a short, simple, and straightforward pattern that stands as an example of how these prayers are expressed in the Psalms. Psalm 13 teaches us how to bring our needs to God in prayer. If we take David's prayer in Psalm 13 as our example, we find six pointers to effective prayer.

First, David speaks directly to God.
The psalmist cries out to God saying,

> ¹ How long, O LORD? Will You forget me forever?
>   How long will You hide Your face from me?

Although we know that everything works for good to them that love God (Romans 8:28), not everything feels good. We are never told in the Bible to ignore these bad things; we are told to take them to God in prayer. In addition to the Psalms, Philippians 4:6 says,

> But in everything with prayer and thanksgiving let your requests be made known unto God; and the peace of God that passes all understanding will keep your heart and mind through Christ Jesus.

Paul exhorts us to take everything—every need, every trial, every burden—unto God in prayer.

Psalm 13 begins like many other prayer psalms by speaking directly to God. Unlike some psalms that speak only *about* God, the laments speak *to* God. It is one thing to talk about God, but it is another thing to talk to God. David says directly to God, "How long, oh Lord, will you forget me? Forever?" (v. 1). So the prayers in the book of Psalms start out speaking directly to God. Sometimes it is helpful to share our burdens with our pastor, our family, and other believers, but sharing with other people cannot take the place of prayer. There is no valid substitute for fervent prayer. Other laments also begin with the psalmist addressing God pointedly:

- Psa 28:1 Unto thee will I cry, O Lord my rock

- Psa 61:1 Hear my cry, O God, listen to my prayer

- Psa 64:1 Hear my voice, O God, in my complaint; preserve my life from dread of the enemy

- Psa 69:1 Save me, O God; for the waters are come in unto my soul

- Psa 140:1 Deliver me, O Lord

- Psa 141:1 Lord, I cry unto thee: make haste unto me

- Psa 143:1 Hear my prayer, O Lord

- Psa 130:1 Out of the depths I cry to thee, O Lord!

Second, David expresses the pain of abandonment.

The psalmist feels abandoned, and he pleads with God: "Will You forget me forever?" This second part of the lament makes plain the feeling of not knowing, the feeling of uncertainty. If we do not feel sure about our trials, it is all right to tell God about our doubts because he already knows what is in our hearts.

David feels like God has forgotten about him, even though he knows he has not. He is asking, "Lord, have you forgotten me? Will you forget me forever? How long will this go on?" This is how he is feeling in the presence of the Lord, and he brings an honest statement before him: "How will long will you hide your face from me?" You may have never felt like God was hidden from you; or maybe you have been hiding from God, like Adam did. Most of us at some point have gone through a dark valley where we felt like we could not find God and like our prayers were just bouncing off the ceiling.

Denial of our pain is not an option. Attempting to ignore our problems will not make them go away. The lament psalms encourage us to engage in faithful and legitimate protest to God. When we are in trouble, we should pour out our souls to him in prayer. Consider these biblical examples of prayer:

Third, David states his problem.

The third characteristic of the lament psalm is found in verse two:

² How long will I take counsel in my soul,
>   having sorrow in my heart;
> and how long will my enemy be exalted over me?

David names his problem; he voices his complaint. He is sorrowful because the enemy has gotten the advantage over him. The enemy, however, is not named specifically. When we read, "My enemy is exalted over me", we do not know the identity of the enemy or how the enemy is attacking David. All we know is that David is in sorrow and that he is suffering because of the attacks of the enemy. The psalm is specific enough that we can name the problem, but it is vague enough that we are able to place ourselves in David's place. Thus, we can pray David's prayer and make it our own prayer.

It is common in the Psalms for people to cry out to God and to voice their complaint. For example, in Psalm 55 he said, "My heart is in anguish within me, and the terror of death has fallen upon me"; and in Psalm 64:1 he pleads, "preserve me from the dread of the enemy". In Psalm 69 he prays, "Save me, oh God; the waters have come up unto my soul". In Psalm 120 he said, "In my distress I cried to the Lord"; and in Psalm 142 he said, "I pour out my complaint before God". In Psalm 107 they cry unto the Lord in their trouble; and Psalm 130 said, "Out of the depths I cried unto the Lord". Outside the book of Psalms Jonah said in Jonah 2:2, "Out of the belly of hell I cried unto you, oh Lord". In the New Testament in 2 Corinthians 1:5, Paul talks about God comforting us in our trouble. He says, "The sufferings of Christ are in us", we are afflicted, and we endure suffering. In verse eight he says, "We were burdened beyond measure, above strength, so that we despaired even of life itself". Paul was so burdened that he thought he was going to die; and he said, "We had the sentence of death, but God delivered us". In 2 Corinthians 12 Paul had a thorn in the flesh, and he said, "I prayed to the Lord three times that it might be removed"; but God said, "My grace is sufficient for you, for my strength is made perfect in weakness"; and Paul said, "So I will glory in my affliction". He brought that burden unto the Lord.

Sorrow and grief are things that are common throughout the Bible. In Matthew 5:4 Jesus said, "Blessed are they that mourn, for they shall be comforted". In James 4 he said, "Lament and mourn and weep; let your laughter be turned to mourning and your joy into gloom, and humble yourselves in the sight of the Lord". Romans

12:15 says, "Rejoice with those that rejoice and weep with those that weep"; and in James 5:13 he said, "Is anyone among you suffering? Let him pray". In Revelation 6, John saw the souls of those that had died under the altar; and they asked, "How long, oh Lord, how long until you judge and avenge our blood on those that dwell on the earth?"

The Psalms of lament give voice to our suffering and our pain. The laments teach us that we should come openly and honestly to God with our needs; we should tell him our doubts and our fears. In doing so, we can be assured that God will not reject us. Jesus declared that God's house should be a house of prayer, but many churches no longer include altar calls, prayer for the sick, and times of seeking the face of God. We have turned worship into entertainment, and we have changed the preaching of the Gospel into self-help sessions and positive thinking philosophy. There is no time given to minister to those who are suffering.

There must be a place among God's people where we can weep with those that weep. When we come to church, some people are ready to rejoice and praise the Lord; but other people are in the bottom of the pit, and they need someone to pray with them. They need to be able to come down to the altar and weep and cry and get help by calling on God. Somehow we must make room for all of that in our church. It would not be appropriate for us to make every church service like a funeral, but neither is it right for us to ignore the needs of those who are suffering.

Many of our brothers and sisters come to church after having received a disconcerting report from the doctor. The people of the church should gather around these and pray for them. Others arrive at church bearing a heavy burden of grief. During times of prayer at the altar, the body of Christ can to respond to their pain, so that grieving ones are not alone in that moment. As they mourn and grieve, we as brothers and sisters should join with them, mourn with them, and weep with them.

Fourth, David pleads for God's intervention.

David has expressed the pain that he is suffering and he has stated his complaint. Now he pleads with God to come to his aid. He says to God,

³ Consider *and* hear me, O LORD my God;
　　Enlighten my eyes, Lest I sleep the *sleep of* death;
⁴ Lest my enemy say, "I have prevailed against him";
　　Lest those who trouble me rejoice when I am moved

He brings his specific need to God and says, "God, I need your help". David is not whining, grumbling, or murmuring. God does not honor the grumblings of complainers. Look at the example of the Israelites in the wilderness when God rained down manna from heaven; and they started grumbling and complaining, "We"re getting tired of this manna". David's prayer is different from the complaining of the Israelites—he has a legitimate need. He is suffering real pain, and he appeals to God saying, "O God, hear my prayer. Consider me and hear me".

Fifth, David trusts God.
David's urgent and passionate prayer is based on a relationship of trust. He says to God,

⁵ But I have trusted in your mercy;
　　My heart shall rejoice in your salvation.

Even though David does not know why he is suffering, he knows that somehow God is in control of things.

The psalmist's confession of trust in God signals a transition from lament to praise. Notice that in verse five David's prayer turns in a different direction. He had come to God; he had talked about his feelings of being abandoned; he had laid out his complaint and his suffering; and he had prayed a specific prayer. But now he says, "I have trusted in your mercy". This is a declaration of faith and trust in God. David has offered up his complaint and he has faithfully brought his need before God. God hears the kind of prayer that says, "I have trusted in your mercy".

The word "mercy" is a covenant word that suggests a relationship of mutual loyalty. David can trust God because they are walking together in covenant. Time and time again David has experienced God's faithfulness. Just as God delivered David from the mouth of the lion and from the attack of Goliath so he will deliver him from this threat as well.

The second part of verse 5 says, "My heart *shall* rejoice in your salvation". In other words, David is confident that God will to do something. Perhaps he has "prayed through" to victory. Now, in the midst of trouble, he is *not* in a rejoicing mood, but soon he will rejoice again. Today may be Friday, but Sunday is coming. We will not be down all of the time. "Yea, though I walk through the valley of the shadow of death, I will fear no evil" (Psalm 23:4). I may be walking through the valley now, but I will come out of the valley. I will *not* stay in the valley forever. I *will* rejoice! We must pray with full confidence and deep trust in God and his faithfulness.

Sixth and finally, David promises to praise God.

These Psalms of urgent prayer, these laments, are uttered by people who are suffering but who also are fully committed to praise. The lament does not last forever: "Weeping may endure for a night, but joy comes in the morning" (Psalm 30:5). In the last verse, the psalmist says,

> ⁶ I will sing to the LORD,
>   Because He has dealt bountifully with me.

Here, David makes a commitment to "sing unto the Lord". Some of these lament psalms go even further than a promise to sing. They make a promise to bring an offering to the temple, saying something like this: "when the answer comes, I will offer up a sacrifice of praise". That is, "I will go down to the house of God and offer up a thanksgiving sacrifice". In biblical times, the Jews had what they called a thanksgiving offering, and many of these prayer psalms included a "vow of praise". The vow of praise means that when the prayer is answered, the person will go to the temple and will offer up a sacrifice of praise unto God.

These prayer psalms have a kind of progression in them. They start out with an expression of pain—"O, Lord, how long" and "where are you" and "I can not even see you and I can not feel you" and "Lord, help me". The psalmist then moves to an expression of faith, saying, "I know you will help me, I know you will hear me, and I will praise you!". They begin in describing the trouble and they end in confessing God's greatness and God's goodness. Should we pray the same kind of prayers today? Jesus did so—right there on the cross he prayed, "My God, my God, why have you forsaken me?" He prays the prayer from Psalm 22. The Lord Jesus himself prayed this kind of prayer, feeling that forsakenness and feeling like God was far away, that he was nowhere to be found. Yet sometimes we do not know whether we should give voice to our pain or ignore our pain and just praise God for his promises.

On May 17, 2008, I was awakened by a severe pain in the center of my chest. I took two aspirin and soon the pain turned into a feeling of pressure, like someone sitting on my chest. I sat down at my desk, and I tried to pray. But I could not think of any words to say, so leaned back in my chair, closed my eyes and said, "Jesus, Jesus, Jesus". When we cannot say anything else, we can call on Jesus, and he knows what is in our hearts. As I called out his name, I began to realize and to know that I was in touch with Jesus. My heart might be causing me some problems, but Jesus was still on the throne. After a time of prayer and seeking God, he gave me a sense of great peace. I was reminded of David's words, "I shall not die but live and declare the works of the Lord" (Psalm 118:17). I was able to put my trust in Jesus and say, "My heart shall rejoice in your salvation; I will sing unto the Lord". Later in the day, when the symptoms continued, I entered the hospital and eventually had heart surgery. I have now recovered completely.

If we will take things to God in prayer and not try to hide our pain, amazing things will happen. We should never pretend that we need no help. We *do* need help. We need Jesus. We need to call on him, call on his name. Some people want to shout; they want to rejoice, but they do not want to pray. Shouting and rejoicing is an important part of worship, but if we have not really touched Jesus, then we have nothing to shout about. If we have not touched Jesus, if we have not given him our burdens, then once we stop our shouting and go home, the burdens will still be laying heavy upon us. We must give our burdens to Jesus, and then we can shout with liberty in our soul. This kind of urgent prayer has been given a name; we call it "praying through". This is calling upon God until we have touched God and we know that he has heard our prayer. It is not just *saying* a prayer, rather it is praying until that confidence and assurance and trust comes down from heaven. It is praying until we feel like God is saying, "I have heard your prayer and I will act on your behalf". We may not know exactly *what* he will do, but we know that he will do *something*. He may say, "Yes"; he may say, "No"; or he may say, "Wait"; but we are content to rest in God's hands.

Conclusion

The suffering of the righteous

We learn in Psalms 1 and 2 that the righteous are blessed and the wicked are punished. The foundation of our faith is that God rules the world according to divinely established rules and principles. Psalm 13, however, presents the other side of the biblical picture of faith in which the neat, tidy, well-ordered theology of Psalms 1 and 2 gives way to a theology that allows for the realities of life, realities that include struggle, injustice, abuse, doubt, fear, and the testing of our faith.

In Psalm 13:1-2, we hear David pray,

> [1] How long, O Lord? Will You forget me forever?
>   How long will You hide Your face from me?
> [2] How long shall I take counsel in my soul,
>   Having sorrow in my heart daily?
>   How long will my enemy be exalted over me?

Psalm 13 teaches us that the righteous will face suffering, trials, and tests. These prayer psalms reflect the experience of Abraham (Genesis 22:1), Joseph (Genesis 37), David, Job, Jeremiah, the Apostles, and even Jesus himself. During times of pain, Psalm 13 will show us a pattern for praying our way to victory.

Prayer Psalms

The most common type of psalm is the Prayer Psalm, which Bible scholars call "the lament". The lament is the worshiper's cry to God for deliverance from distress. The sufferer's trouble may take the form of sickness (Psalm 6), personal or corporate sin (Psalm 51), oppression (Psalm 10), or an accusation (Psalm 17). The lament usually begins with an address to God, followed by the specific complaint or need. The worshiper may then confess trust in God and offer up a petition to God. The lament may include a declaration of assurance that God has heard the prayer and conclude with a promise to praise God with a thanksgiving offering. Note the following example of the lament (Psalm 54):

> 1. Address to God
>   O God, save me (v. 1)
> 2. Complaint (reason for the prayer)

strangers have risen up against me
and oppressors have sought after my life (v. 3)
3. Confession of trust in God
   Behold, God is my helper (v. 4)
4. Petition for help
   Vindicate me … Hear my prayer (vv. 1-2)
5. Assurance of being heard
   he has delivered me out of all trouble (v. 7)
6. Vow of praise offering
   I will freely sacrifice unto you; I will praise your
   name, O Lord (v. 6).

The Prayer Psalms teach us the importance of being open and honest with God. We have learned in our religious circles to mask our true feelings. When it comes to our relationship with God, the psalms teach us that we can be totally open and honest with God.

Furthermore, the psalms of lament teach us that we should make a place for prayer in our worship services. Many churches have turned worship into nothing but celebration, and they have relegated prayer to the back rooms. Biblical worship provides a time and place for passionate prayer, for crying out to God. The New Testament instructs us to include times of prayer for people in the congregation (James 5.13-18). We are to "be anxious for nothing, but in everything by prayer and supplication, let [our] requests be made known unto God" (Philippians 4.6). Peter says, "casting all your care upon him, because he cares for you" (1 Peter 5.7). The early church prayed together in times of need (Acts 1.14; 2.42; 3.1; 4.31; 6.4, 6; 8.15; 12.5; 13.1-3; 14.23; 16.13, 25; 20.36).

The lament psalms include Psalms 3-7, 9-14, 16, 17, 22, 25-28, 31, 35, 36, 38-40, 42-44, 51-64, 69-71, 74, 77, 79, 80, 83, 85, 86, 88, 90, 94, 102, 106, 108, 109, 120, 123, 126, 130, 137, and 140-143.

We must include prayer as an important part of our worship services. When we come together for worship, not everything we do is praise. We also give testimony to one another, we tell each other what we have been doing, we visit, we encourage one another, we teach, we preach, and we pray. Prayer is a vital component of genuine worship. On any given Sunday, a large portion of any congregation will consist of people who are hurting severely. The most meaningful and helpful thing we can do for them in the service is to reach out to them. They need more than a sermon. They need more than uplifting songs. They need the touch of caring brothers and sisters in Christ. They need a church that will spend time with them in prayer until the Holy Spirit breaks through to victory.

Psalm 13 Personalized

If we find it difficult to say the right words and to speak forth our pain, we might want to use the following exercise as a way of starting the process of urgent prayer. We can write our name where David's name stood. We can write our needs were David's needs were listed. We can list our troubles, our feelings, and our specific request. We can take this version of Psalm 13, our own personal version, and come before God saying, "Here is my need Lord. I am giving my pain to you. Please help me".

A Psalm of _____.
                     (your name)
[1] How long, O LORD? Will You forget me forever?
    How long will You hide Your face from me?
[2] How long _____
                      (tell your trouble)

    Having _____ in my heart daily?
         (express your painful feeling)

    How long will _____?
              (restate your suffering)

[3] Consider and hear me, O LORD my God;

_____

               (state your prayer to God)

[4] Lest my enemy say, "I have prevailed against him";
    Lest those who trouble me rejoice when I am moved.
[5] But I have trusted in Your mercy;
    My heart shall rejoice in Your salvation.
[6] I will sing to the LORD,
    Because He has dealt bountifully with me.

Whenever we have a burden in our heart, and we put together the right words, we should open up the book of Psalms and read through the prayers. In the psalms we will find a prayer that will express our pain. We can make the psalm our own personal prayer God will honor it. The psalms are God's word; they are prayers of David and of other saints of God. And we can make them *our* prayers. Then, in addition to this help from the psalmist, we must submit ourselves to the Holy Spirit, who will pray through us "with groanings that cannot be uttered" (Rom. 8.26).

Chapter 3

God's Presence
in the Midst of Pain

Psalm 22
To the Chief Musician. Set to "The Deer of the Dawn".
A Psalm of David.
¹ My God, my God, why have You forsaken me?
   Why are You so far from helping me,
   And from the words of my groaning?
² O my God, I cry in the daytime, but You do not hear;
   And in the night season, and am not silent.
³ But You *are* holy,
   Enthroned in the praises of Israel.
⁴ Our fathers trusted in You;
   They trusted, and You delivered them.
⁵ They cried to You, and were delivered;
   They trusted in You, and were not ashamed.
⁶ But I *am* a worm, and no man;
   A reproach of men, and despised by the people.
⁷ All those who see me ridicule me;
   They shoot out the lip, they shake the head, *saying,*
⁸ "He trusted in the Lord, let Him rescue Him;
   Let Him deliver Him, since He delights in Him!"
⁹ But You *are* He who took me out of the womb;
   You made me trust *while* on my mother's breasts.
¹⁰ I was cast upon You from birth.
   From my mother's womb You *have been* my God.

¹¹ Be not far from me, For trouble *is* near;
> For *there is* none to help.
¹² Many bulls have surrounded me;
> Strong *bulls* of Bashan have encircled me.
¹³ They gape at me *with* their mouths,
> *Like* a raging and roaring lion.
¹⁴ I am poured out like water,
> And all my bones are out of joint;
> My heart is like wax; It has melted within me.
¹⁵ My strength is dried up like a potsherd,
> And my tongue clings to my jaws;
> You have brought me to the dust of death.
¹⁶ For dogs have surrounded me;
> The congregation of the wicked has enclosed me.
> They pierced my hands and my feet;
¹⁷ I can count all my bones.
> They look *and* stare at me.
¹⁸ They divide my garments among them,
> And for my clothing they cast lots.
¹⁹ But You, O LORD, do not be far from me;
> O my Strength, hasten to help me!
²⁰ Deliver me from the sword,
> My precious *life* from the power of the dog.
²¹ Save me from the lion's mouth
> And from the horns of the wild oxen!
> You have answered me.
²² I will declare Your name to my brethren;
> In the midst of the assembly I will praise You.
²³ You who fear the LORD, praise Him!
> All you descendants of Jacob, glorify Him,
> And fear Him, all you offspring of Israel!
²⁴ For He has not despised nor abhorred
> the affliction of the afflicted;
> Nor has He hidden His face from him;
> But when He cried to him, He heard.
²⁵ My praise *shall be* of You in the great assembly;
> I will pay my vows before those who fear Him.
²⁶ The poor shall eat and be satisfied;
> Those who seek Him will praise the LORD.

Let your heart live forever!
[27] All the ends of the world
    Shall remember and turn to the LORD,
    And all the families of the nations
    Shall worship before You.
[28] For the kingdom *is* the LORD's,
    And He rules over the nations.
[29] All the prosperous of the earth Shall eat and worship;
    All those who go down to the dust Shall bow before Him,
    Even he who cannot keep himself alive.
[30] A posterity shall serve Him.
    It will be recounted of the Lord to the *next* generation,
[31] They will come and declare His righteousness
    to a people who will be born,
    That He has done *this*.

Psalm 22 might be called "Pain, Praises, and the Passion of Christ". The Psalm is quoted in the New Testament in relation to the crucifixion of Jesus. At Calvary Jesus endured great pain as he suffered for the sins of the world. As he hung upon the cross, suspended as a mediator between heaven and earth, he cried out to his heavenly father, "My God, my God, why have you forsaken me" (Matthew 27:46; Mark 15:34). Jesus took the words of his ancestor David and appropriated them to his own hour of pain. These words cited by Jesus, words of the ancient psalmist, cause us to ask the question, "Where is God when we are suffering?"

Introduction

Psalm 22 follows the same pattern of urgent prayer as Psalm 13. It can be outlined in two parts: the first part is prayer (vv. 1-21a), and the second part is praise (vv. 21b-31). At the end of his prayer, the psalmist professes his faith, saying, "You have answered me" (v. 21). We do not know how he comes to that conclusion. We do not know exactly what the process was except that somehow, in coming to God in prayer and in seeking the Lord, he comes to the conclusion that God had heard his prayer. Even though nothing has changed, the psalmist changes from prayer to praise. As we take a look at this powerful Psalm, we will learn how to move from prayer to praise.

A Psalm of Pain

David feels forsaken.

Before reaching the place of praise, David expresses his feeling of pain that God has not answered him. He says,

> [1] My God, my God, why have You forsaken me?
>> *Why are You so* far from helping me,
>> *And from* the words of my groaning?
> [2] O my God, I cry in the daytime, but You do not hear;
>> And in the night season, and am not silent.

The psalmist feels like he has been forsaken. He knows that God is everywhere present, yet God has not intervened to help him. Therefore, he feels deserted by God. David is in trouble, yet God has not delivered him, and he feels like he has been left to fend for himself. He faces a deep sense of aloneness.

The lamenting cry of David is deep and piercing, and yet it is not a cry of complete despair and hopelessness. He begins his prayer in a way that suggests a longing and yearning to be in the presence of his God. He uses the phrase "my God, my God". He is calling upon the God of whom he sings, "The Lord is my shepherd, I shall not want" (Psalm 23:1). He is crying out to the God who protects him through the "valley of the shadow of death" and who comforts him with his rod and staff (Psalm 23:4). He is David's provider who "prepares a table" before him even in the presence of his enemies, who anoints his head with oil, and who makes his cup to run over (Psalm 23:5). David's desire is to live forever in God's presence—to "dwell in the house of the Lord forever" (Psalm 23:6). When David cries out "my God, my God", he is seeking divine aid from the God who delivered him from the lion and the bear, who saved him the mighty Goliath, and who protected him from the armies of the Philistines and from those of Saul. David is pleading with his God, who had brought him from the sheepfold and had made him king over Israel.

David's lament to God is not uttered in an attitude of doubt. David does not wonder if God is real or if God is able to help. His prayer is an attempt to convince God to intervene, to act. He is saying to God, "You have saved me in the past, please save me again now."

David's payer reminds me of Luke 18:1, where Jesus "spoke unto them a parable that men ought always to pray and not faint", that is, they should not give up on praying. He told the story of a woman whose rights were being violated, and she brought her case to a judge. The judge would not help her, but she kept on coming coming back again and again. Jesus says something like this, "I tell you what this unjust judge will do, he cares not about this woman or her need, but because of her persistence, he will do what she asks". And Jesus then said, "how much more should your father in heaven, who loves you, and care for you, answer the prayer of the one who calls upon him. I tell you he will answer them quickly" (Luke 18:1-8). David is praying this kind of persistent prayer. And it is this kind of persistent and urgent prayer that God hears and answers.

Another example that we might point to is the woman who came to Jesus whose daughter was possessed by an evil spirit. The disciples told her to be quiet. They told her that she was not a Jew and she should leave Jesus alone. They said, "You are a Gentile, and we don't minister to your kind." But she kept crying out, and finally, Jesus asked, "What do you want?" She replied, "My daughter is grievously vexed with a devil." And he said, "Go your way; your daughter is healed." And he turned to his disciples and he said, "I have not seen so great faith, no not in Israel" (Matthew 15:22-28). It was because of her persistence that Jesus stood still and turned and answered her prayer. God is looking for people who will cry out to him from the midst of their pain.

God had not answered the psalmist, but he continued to pray in the daytime and in the nighttime. He did not give up hope. When we have been in trouble and God has not delivered us, do we continue to pray? Do we cry out to God night and day for his help, or do we only spend our time complaining to our friends and your family. Friends and family are important as support and as encouragers, but only God can make a difference. If we have not been crying out to God in the daytime and in the nighttime, then we cannot expect God to act.

David remembers that God has answered others.

Here in verses 3-5, David looks back to the testimonies of his ancestors in the faith. The psalmist is crying out around-the-clock, and then he remembers what God has done for his father, for his mother, and for his church. He declares to the Lord,

³ But You *are* holy,
    Enthroned in the praises of Israel.
⁴ Our fathers trusted in You;
    They trusted, and You delivered them.
⁵ They cried to You, and were delivered;
    They trusted in You, and were not ashamed.

David is feeling abandoned, and it seems that his prayer has not been heard. Nevertheless, without wavering he continues to affirm the holy character of God. The delay in the answer of David's prayers is not due to a lack of goodness or righteousness on God's part, for God is holy. Furthermore, David's feelings of abandonment are not due to God's impotence, for God is Israel's king, who sits enthroned on the praises of Israel. Verse 3, which is often quoted in the Church, proclaims that the holy God inhabits the praises of his people Israel.

We remember from Psalm 13 that the psalms of lament almost always have a reference to trust, and we notice that the theme of trust is repeated here in Psalm 22:4-5. David says, "Our fathers trusted in you, and you delivered. They cried and were delivered. They trusted and they were not ashamed". In effect, the psalmist says, "Now I am trusting God. I am trusting as my ancestors trusted. And I expect to have the same response to my prayers."

Opposition is on every side.

After his expression of trust in the Lord, David restates his problem. It seems that he is surrounded by opposition and oppressed by persecutors. He cries mournfully,

⁶ But I *am* a worm, and no man;
    A reproach of men, and despised by the people.

[7] All those who see me ridicule me;

They shoot out the lip, they shake the head, *saying,*

[8] "He trusted in the LORD, let Him rescue him;

Let Him deliver him, since He delights in him!"

We do not know the identity of the psalmist's opposition, but he is clearly facing desertion not only from God but also from the people around him. He says, "I am a worm, I am a reproach; I am despised; I am ridiculed". Here is a person who is rejected. The psalmist is remembering what God has done in the past. God saved his people; God has answered prayer. But now, the people who should come to his aid are not helping him, instead, they are abusing him. He is alone in the midst of a crowd. No one is helping David, and in fact, everyone is ridiculing him. We all feel like that at times—alone in the midst of a crowd. We attend church, but feel isolated, discouraged, despondent, with no one to help.

David's plight reminds us of Job, whose friends should have been encouraging him and praying for him, but instead they are accusing him. They say, "if you had been a good man, these tragedies would never have happened to you. Surely, you must have sinned against God, and he is punishing you." This kind of judgmental behavior continues to happen in the Church. Christians who are suffering from sickness or tragedy are often accused of bringing the trouble upon themselves by their unbelief or by their disobedience. Faithful and dedicated Christians are subject to sickness and suffering just like everyone else.

David has relied upon God from birth.

In the face of ridicule and opposition, the psalmist recalls the grace of God in earlier days. David declares that he had served God all the days of his life. He says,

[9] But You *are* He who took me out of the womb;

You made me trust *while* on my mother's breasts.

[10] I was cast upon You from birth.

From my mother's womb You *have been* my God.

David claims that God has cared for him from the moment that emerged from the womb. When he was nursing at his mother's breasts, the Lord cared for him. He testifies that from birth God has been a reality in his life. God has been with him and has provided for him.

Threats are all around.

In verses 11-13, the psalmist again sets forth his desperate situation. Many enemies are circling around him, and he compares his opposers to animals. He prays for Gods help saying,

¹¹ Be not far from me, For trouble *is* near;
　　For *there is* none to help.
¹² Many bulls have surrounded me;
　　Strong *bulls* of Bashan have encircled me.
¹³ They gape at me *with* their mouths,
　　Like a raging and roaring lion.

His enemies are so dreadful that they are like animals. They are like angry, ravenous beasts. He pleads with God saying, "Be not far from me, for trouble is near, and there is none to help." David's God seems far off, but his trouble is close at hand, and he needs help. Who are these enemies? They are bulls and they are lions. Angry people are encircling him like strong bulls. Also, like lions, ravenous people are gaping and roaring at him with their mouths.

Life seems to be falling apart.

Not only is David surrounded by danger, but his body itself is deteriorating rapidly. He is so sick and so afflicted that he feels like his whole life is falling apart. He reveals his pain saying,

¹⁴ I am poured out like water,
　　And all my bones are out of joint;
　　My heart is like wax; It has melted within me.
¹⁵ My strength is dried up like a potsherd,
　　And my tongue clings to my jaws;
　　You have brought me to the dust of death.

We do not know if the original writer is physically ill, or if his references to illness are metaphors that signify the painful effects of the opposition that he is facing. Sometimes we may not be physically ill, but emotionally we feel like we could die. We feel sick because we are dealing with something that is draining and devastating.

So the psalmist says, "I am poured out like water". It is as if his energy, his life force, is being drained. Have you ever received a troubling phone call, or a disaster happened, and you seem to feel your life draining from your body?

The psalmist adds, "all of my bones are out of joint; my heart is like wax; my strength is dried up; my tongue sticks to my jaws; you have brought me to the dust of death." David feels like he is dying—his strength is exhausted and his life is fading away.

People are waiting for him to die.

And then, those that are around are just talking about what will happen when he dies.

¹⁶ For dogs have surrounded me;

    The assembly of the wicked has enclosed me.

    They pierced my hands and my feet;

¹⁷ I can count all my bones.

    They look *and* stare at me.

¹⁸ They divide my garments among them,

    And for my clothing they cast lots.

"Dogs have surrounded me", he says. First it was bulls, then lions, now dogs. These dogs are "an assembly of the wicked". After circling around him, these dogs have pierced his hands and his feet. In the original context of the Psalm, the meaning would be that the dogs are biting David's hands and feet. Their long fangs are piercing through the flesh. The writer of Matthew's Gospel sees this verse fulfilled at the cross when the hands and feet of Jesus were pierced by the nails.

The acuteness of the psalmist's condition is pressed further by his statement "I can count all my bones." It seems that his body has wasted away because of illness or because he has been unable to procure food. For whatever reason, however, he is nothing but skin and bones.

Onlookers stand by awaiting his death. In anticipation of his approaching demise, they begin to divide up his garments among themselves, and they cast lots for his clothing. These gawkers would not be members of his family because the family would follow established guidelines for dispensing of the deceased's personal property. Again, the Gospel of Matthew picks up this psalm and applies it to Jesus. As Jesus died upon the cross, the Roman soldiers who had carried out the death sentence of crucifixion cast lots for his seamless robe.

A Psalm of Prayer

David cries out to God.

While David's enemies are circling around him and waiting for him to die, wondering how they can profit from his death, David chooses to turn his gaze away from his enemies and back toward God. Even when facing desperate circumstances, believers can choose where to focus their attention. The psalmist chooses to focus again upon God and to cry out in prayer. Pleading for divine intervention, his prayer is this:

¹⁹ But You, O LORD, do not be far from me;
  O my Strength, hasten to help me!
²⁰ Deliver me from the sword,
  My precious *life* from the power of the dog.
²¹ Save me from the lion's mouth
  And from the horns of the wild oxen!
  You have answered me.

The psalmist has painted a gruesome picture of his critical situation. And now he puts into words an urgent petition, a pointed prayer. His request is "O Lord, do not be far from me, O my strength. Hasten to help me." Knowing that his end is near at hand, David urges God to hurry. There is no time to lose. The situation is looking hopeless, and he needs God to intervene immediately. He prays that God will deliver him from the power of the sword and the dog. He asks that God will save him from the lion's mouth and from the horns of the wild oxen. The animals spoken up here are a repetition from the previous verses, but here they are in reverse order.

David then makes an amazing statement at the end of verse 21. He proclaims, "You have answered me." Suddenly, David lays claim to God's promises and declares his assurance that God has heard his prayer.

David promises a sacrifice of praise.

David's assurance that God has heard his prayer moves him to make two promises. First, he promises to testify to his brethren. Second, he promises to offer a thanksgiving sacrifice in the temple. These two promises are really just two parts of one event. When David comes to the temple to offer his sacrifice of praise, he will share his testimony of how God brought him out of trouble.

[22] I will declare Your name to my brethren;
> In the midst of the assembly I will praise You.
[23] You who fear the LORD, praise Him!
> All you descendants of Jacob, glorify Him,
> And fear Him, all you offspring of Israel!
[24] For He has not despised nor abhorred
> the affliction of the afflicted;
> Nor has He hidden His face from Him;
> But when He cried to Him, He heard.
[25] My praise *shall be* of You in the great assembly;
> I will pay my vows before those who fear Him.
[26] The poor shall eat and be satisfied;
> Those who seek Him will praise the LORD.
> Let your heart live forever!

Not only does David promise to praise the Lord, but he also calls upon the people to offer up praise. He invites the people saying, "all of you who fear the Lord, praise him, praise him." Is the psalmist saying that they should praise God because things are better now? No, David's situation is not yet better. Is he asking the people to praise God because the trouble is over? No, the trouble is not over yet. Instead, David is urging the people to praise God because he knows that God has heard his prayer. God has the answer, and he is on the way to intervene and to deliver. A similar perspective is taken in the New Testament by John, who writes, "whatever things you desire when you pray, believe that you received them and you shall have them." Both David and John understood the truth that when we pray in faith, God responds. So the psalmist declares, "I believe that God has heard my prayer, so let us praise him!"

But praying in faith is not so simple as it sounds. To pray with faith demands more than simply repeating a Scripture promise over and over. It requires more than words and confessions and making claims upon God. The process of finding assurance in prayer is what many of us have called "praying through". This process is difficult to explain and it is difficult to learn. The best way to learn how to pray through is to spend time praying alongside a person who is experienced in the process. We must learn from them, and we must look at their example. To pray through like David prayed means that we pour out our hearts to God and express honestly our deepest needs. It means that we cry out for God's help. It means that we look back and remember what God has done in the past, and it means that we express our trust in God for the present time.

To pray through means that we wrestle with God like Jacob and that we refuse to let go of God until he promises to deliver us. Somewhere during this process, the Holy Spirit works in our hearts to give us an assurance that God has heard our prayers. That assurance can come many different ways. Most of the time it is just a feeling of peace that comes over us. There might be times when we open up the Bible and we read a verse and we know that this verse is meant for us. With a still small voice, God might speak to us in our minds. Or we may have a dream, or we may receive another kind of miraculous sign. There many different ways that God speaks to us to give us that assurance.

Psalm 22 holds together that tension between crying out to God in prayer and praising God for the answer. In our worship we must choose which approach to take. At any given moment we must choose either prayer or praise. Psalm 22 teaches us that we must do both. We must pray with urgency, with passion, with determination, and with faith. But we must also, after we have prayed, express our trust in God and offer up to him a sacrifice of praise. Normally, we begin with prayer and move from there into praise.

Notice the last line where the psalmist says, "I will pay my vows". In the biblical times people often made vows to God in hopes they would move him to hear their petitions. For example, we read in the Psalms that the psalmists would make a vow to offer a sacrifice. They would say to God, "When you have answered my prayer I will come to the temple and offer up a sacrifice of praise." This sacrifice of praise is a thanksgiving offering.

David expands his praise.

When David moves from prayer to praise, he first focuses upon his own praise. He promises to praise God with a sacrifice. Then he calls upon the congregation to give praise to God. Now, in verse 27 he expands his call to all inhabitants of the earth. He invites everyone to join in with him, saying,

[27] All the ends of the world
> Shall remember and turn to the LORD,
> And all the families of the nations
> Shall worship before You.
[28] For the kingdom *is* the LORD's,
> And He rules over the nations.
[29] All the prosperous of the earth shall eat and worship;
> All those who go down to the dust
>> shall bow before Him,
> Even he who cannot keep himself alive.
[30] A posterity shall serve Him.
> It will be recounted of the Lord
>> to the *next* generation,
[31] They will come and declare His righteousness
> to a people who will be born,
> That He has done *this*.

David declares that the entire world, the "ends of the earth" will turn to the Lord; all the "families of the nations" will worship the Lord. The reason that the people of the nations will come to worship God is that the "kingdom is the Lord's". The Lord rules over the nations. Those who are alive and prospering will worship God, and even those who have died will bow down before him. David's words foreshadow the claims of the apostle Paul, who writes, "every knee shall bow … and every tongue shall confess" (Philippians 2:10-11).

Looking into the future, David sees that even after we die, our posterity, our children, our descendents will serve God (v. 30). The next generation will declare his righteousness to a people yet to be born. Generation after generation will be hearing about the works of the Lord.

The psalmist concludes Psalm 22 with the powerful affirmation that the coming generations will know that it is Lord who has been at work in our lives—"He has done this". God has done this. David promises to testify and tell other generations what God has done. Some of us have grown up in Christian families and have grown up in church, but still we have not heard the testimonies of the mighty works of God. We focus so much on the present that we forget to tell our children and grandchildren what God has done for us in the past. It is God's works in the past to provide a foundation for the future.

In my family, and the church that I grew up in, there was no emphasis on testimony, and I did not know the stories of the past. My parents and grandparents were Christians but I'd never heard of any great works that God had done in their lives. In fact, my grandfather was a Baptist preacher, but I know nothing about the events of his ministry.

My grandmother was more talkative, but she rarely spoke of spiritual things. I finally caught a glimpse of her faith when she was about 90 years old (she lived to be 105). I went to visit her, and she offered to make lunch (I loved her biscuits). We were standing in the kitchen; she was sifting her flour, and we were talking. She began to speak to me in a whisper, almost as if she was telling me a deep secret that she was afraid to make known. She said to me,

> I know that your church believes in praying for the sick, but we never did that. But I will tell you something that I've never told anybody else. When I was a little girl, I was 12 years old, and my mother got sick, and everybody said she was going to die. She was laying in the bed, dying, and all the family had gone to bed, and we were waiting on mama to die. I got up out of the bed and I went down to mama's room, and I knelt down beside her bed. I began to pray, and I said Jesus, I've been told that you don't work miracles anymore, but I need a miracle today. If you are real then please heal my mama. And I don't know if it was my prayer or something else but Mama was healed and she was able to get out of bed and she fully recovered.

As I reflect upon my grandmother's story, I would note that it reports a marvelous miracle of God's healing power. But also, I wonder why my family, my grandmother in particular, did not realize how valuable the story could be. We need to tell our children what God has done for us. We need to tell those that are born the wonderful works of God. We need to tell those who are young and old, "this is what the Lord has done". The Jews continue to observe the Passover in order to share from generation to generation the experience of the exodus from Egypt. The Church continues to celebrate the Lord's Supper in order to re-experience the atoning death of Jesus on the cross. The Lord's Supper is a way of telling everyone that Jesus died on the cross and his blood is still efficacious for the forgiveness of sins. The bread is the body of Christ, and the wine is the blood of Christ. Beyond these rituals, we should regularly report to our children what God has done. Through our testimonies they learn that God is real, and as they grow up, they will be strengthened as they rely upon the testimonies of their elders.

Conclusion

Psalm 22 is appropriate for any believer, at any time in history from David until now. Like David, we can approach God in our times of pain and call upon him saying, "God I need your help, I'm surrounded, I feel like I'm dying, I feel like I need you Lord, my life is falling apart, I need you to help me." This Psalm is appropriate for the faithful, for God's people who are suffering.

And that is why Jesus appropriated it for himself—it reflects the depth of despair and suffering that he endured upon the cross. The Gospel of Mark reports that Jesus, while hanging upon the cross, uttered the words of the psalmist: "My God, my God, why have you forsaken me?" (Mark 15:34). Jesus, being steeped in the Old Testament, is able to take this verse and apply it to the suffering that he was going through.

When Jesus says, "My God, my God, why have you forsaken me?", he is not asking for information.It is a rhetorical question that is meant not to require an answer. The question is an expression of pain. The word "Why?" is a way of asking God to reveal his presence. Jesus is not really asking, "Why?" He knew why. He knew the reason. It is not a question of asking for information, it is the expression of suffering that identifies with the psalmist David. Jesus, the son of David, appropriates the words of David, laying claim to the Scripture that was written hundreds of years before. Later, the disciples of Jesus look back to Psalm 22 and they see other correspondences between the words of the psalm and the events of the crucifixion. Like David, Jesus was surrounded by enemies and he suffered rejection by his people.

When Jesus quotes Psalm 22:1, he expresses the awful reality of the cross. Jesus was not imagining the pain. It was genuine pain. It was real suffering. He was really dying. His life was really going out of him. His heart was really breaking. His bones were really showing. It was real. It was not imaginary. Jesus identifies with his people who had suffered in the past and who had sung this psalm for hundreds of years.

Also, this psalm tells us that the problem on the cross was the sin of humanity. Jesus is surrounded by his own people, the Jews who rejected him. They turned against him, and his affliction is because of the sin of humanity. He is bearing the total sin and rebellion of all humanity. Here in the center of Psalm 22, verses 11 through 18, we read about the rejection of the people. There are powerful forces at work, all attempting to destroy Jesus: the governor, Herod, the Sanhedrin court, the ruling Jews, the religious people. These people are attacking Jesus, while they should be supporting Jesus.

It is easy to connect verses 9 and 10 to the life of Jesus as well. From birth, from his mother's womb, he trusted God. When choosing the mother who would bear his son, God found a humble woman who trusted the Lord. Jesus, the son of God, was taught and raised by a young woman named Mary. She taught him to trust in the Lord. His earthly father Joseph taught him the same.

Why did Jesus quote from Psalm 22? One reason was to bring that Psalm to all those who were listening to him around the cross and to all of us who would read the Gospels. When he quoted from Psalm 22, he brought the psalm to the people, because even in his death, Jesus had in mind the people who were listening. He even cared about the thief that was beside him on the other cross. And one of his last words was "Father forgive them for they know not what they do". Jesus did not go to the cross feeling sorry for himself, rather, he went to the cross out of love lost for humanity. He spoke the words of Psalm 22 in order to say to us, "This Psalm points to me". His quotation of Psalm 22 suggests that everything that happened in Psalm 22 was happening on the cross, and we are all witnesses.

Chapter 4

Building Faith

through Songs of Trust

Psalm 27
A Psalm of David.
[1] The LORD is my light and my salvation;
        Whom shall I fear?
        The LORD is the strength of my life;
        Of whom shall I be afraid?
[2] When the wicked came against me to eat up my flesh,
        My enemies and foes, they stumbled and fell.
[3] Though an army may encamp against me,
        My heart shall not fear;
        Though war should rise against me,
        I am trusting in this.
[4] One thing I have desired of the LORD, that will I seek:
        That I may dwell in the house of the LORD
        All the days of my life,
        To behold the beauty of the LORD,
        And to inquire in His temple.
[5] For in the time of trouble
        He shall hide me in His pavilion;
        In the secret place of His tabernacle
                He shall hide me;
        He shall set me high upon a rock.
[6] And now my head shall be lifted up
        above my enemies all around me;

Therefore I will offer sacrifices of joy
    in His tabernacle;
    I will sing, yes, I will sing praises to the LORD.
[7] Hear, O LORD, when I cry with my voice!
    Have mercy also upon me, and answer me.
[8] When You said, "Seek My face,"
    My heart said to You, "Your face, LORD, I will seek."
[9] Do not hide Your face from me;
    Do not turn Your servant away in anger;
    You have been my help;
    Do not leave me nor forsake me,
        O God of my salvation.
[10] When my father and my mother forsake me,
    Then the LORD will take care of me.
[11] Teach me Your way, O LORD,
    And lead me in a smooth path,
        because of my enemies.
[12] Do not deliver me to the will of my adversaries;
    For false witnesses have risen against me,
    And such as breathe out violence.
[13] I would have lost heart, unless I had believed
    That I would see the goodness of the LORD
    In the land of the living.
[14] Wait on the LORD; be of good courage,
    And He shall strengthen your heart;
    Wait, I say, on the LORD!

How important is our trust in God? In light of the uncertainties surrounding us in the contemporary world, Christians must learn to put their complete trust in God and in his grace. The world economy is in a shambles; terrorism continues to threaten any hopes for global peace; new drug resistant diseases endanger our health; and frequent natural disasters challenge our ability to maintain a stable and effective society. Undoubtedly, unbelievers will be suspicious, skeptical, and pessimistic; but Christians must rise to the occasion and confess our trust in God. God has not vacated his throne, and he has not been stripped of his sovereignty. To trust God means that we accept God at his word and that we put ourselves in unreservedly into his hands.

The Psalms of Trust

When we think of the Psalms, we usually think of praise, but there are many kinds of Psalms. The most common type of psalm is the psalm of prayer or lament, in which the psalmist is encountering some form of trouble. In the laments, the psalmist is in trouble, needing help from God, and he calls upon God. He cries out to God for his help. Those psalms of urgent prayer are the most common type of psalm within the book of Psalms. In the midst of their praying and in the midst of their crying out to God, they would come to a place where they would profess complete trust in the Lord. Even though the storm is still raging, the psalmist declares, "I will trust in the Lord". Even though the waters are rising, he says, "I will trust in the Lord". Even though the enemy has come against him, he insists, "I will trust in the Lord". It is that trust, that faith, that sustains the psalmist in the time of need. He grasps hold of God to keep him safe in the midst of the storm.

I am reminded of the old song that says,

Till the storm passes over,
    till the thunder sounds no more,
    till the clouds roll forever from the sky,
Hold me fast, let me stand,
    in the hollow of your hand,
Keep me safe till the storm passes by.

When the storm is raging, we must hold fast to the anchor, Jesus Christ. He is the anchor of our soul. We must hold fast to him and keep our trust in him. The Psalms do not tell us to trust in the Lord only when things are going well. Genuine trust in the Lord is found when things are not going well, yet we have determined in our hearts that what our eyes see and what our heart feels is not everything. The future is not determined by our senses and our circumstances. Our future is in the hands of God. He is working behind the scenes, and we must put our trust in him.

The profession of trust is an important element in the psalms of lament. The following psalms of lament include a brief statement of trust in the Lord:

Psalm 4:5 "… put your trust in the Lord"

Psalm 5:11 "let all those who put their trust in you rejoice"

Psalm 7:1 "O Lord my God, in you do I put my trust"

Psalm 13:5 "but I have trusted in your mercy"

Psalm 17:7 "O you who save by your right hand them which put their trust in you"

Psalm 22:4 "Our fathers trusted in you: they trusted, and you delivered them"

These and many other examples demonstate that the confession of trust is an important element within the prayer psalms (psalms of lament). The profession of trust, which is no more than a single statement in many psalms, here becomes an entire psalm. Thus, in Psalm 27, the confession of trust is transformed from its role as one small part of the lament psalm to create a new type of psalm, the psalm of trust. Unlike the psalms of lament, Psalm 27 is not uttered during a time of suffering. The psalmist does not express a specific need. His only prayer is for the continuation of God's presence in his life. Neither does he come to God with a specific item of thanksgiving. That is, he does not point back to a particular event for which he is giving thanks. Many of the psalms focus on one thing for which the psalmist gives thanks or praise, one act of deliverance, or one event in the life of the psalmist. Many of the psalms focus on giving praise for the deliverance from the exodus, others praise God for his role as creator, or for his role as king. But this psalm, Psalm 27, does not have a focus on prayer or praise. This psalm focuses on trust and faith. In it the psalmist says, "In whatever situation I find myself, I have determined that I will trust in the Lord".

Given the battles that we fight today, the opposition that we face, and the challenges that are before us, the attitude of trust that is exemplified in Psalm 27 is an attitude and posture that is vital for our survival. It is essential that God's people learn to trust God. We need to realize and understand that whatever goes on in the economy, we can trust the Lord to be our provider. Whatever goes on in the government, we can trust the Lord to be our guide. Whatever goes on in our community, we can trust in the Lord to be our protection. Whatever goes on with our health, we can trust the Lord is our healer. Whatever is going on with our family or on our job, we can trust in the Lord to be our strength. We do not trust in what humans can do. We do not trust what the government can do for us or what our boss can do for us. We must learn to trust in the Lord.

Psalm 27: A Song of Trust

Theology—Who is God?

At the heart of this psalm is a deep theology of worship. Many Christians do not have a very good opinion of theologians or of theology, and the reason for this negative opinion of theology is that theologians talk in a language that only they understand. But the Psalms are also theology, yet they present theology in a different kind of language. The Psalms are the theology of the people and a theology that reflects a personal relationship with God. The writers of the Psalms express the importance of God for their own lives and for the life of their congregation. Psalm 27:1 says,

[1] The LORD is my light and my salvation;
> Whom shall I fear?
The LORD is the strength of my life;
> Of whom shall I be afraid?

"The Lord is…"—this is a statement of theology. When we attempt to describe God, we are expressing our theology. But unlike traditional theology, which describes God in abstract philosophical terms, the Psalms use concrete metaphorical terms. A theologian might say that God is "eternally existent, self-sufficient, omnipotent, omniscient, and omnipresent." But David says, "The Lord is my light … the Lord is my salvation." Is God eternal? Of course, but he is our light. And is God omniscient? Of course, but he is our salvation. Is God omnipresent? Of course, but he is the strength of our lives. When it is dark, and we need a light, and the Lord is our light. When we cannot see the path in front of us, he shines the light on our pathway. The Lord is our light. The Lord is our salvation. When we are in trouble, he saves us. When we have a need, he delivers us. The Lord is our light, and the Lord is our salvation. The Lord is the strength of our lives. When we are weak, in him we are strong. When we are facing a Goliath in our lives, we can turn to the strength of the Lord, and we can say to the giant, "You come against me with a sword and with a spear, but I come to you in the name of the Lord of hosts." "The Lord is the strength of my life, of whom shall I be afraid." The Psalms are deeply theological, but it is a theology expressed in the language of worship and in the language of the common person.

God is the strength of those who trust him.
When David says, "The Lord is my light", he is making a theological statement. When he says, "The Lord is the strength of my life, of whom shall I be afraid", he is constructing and confessing his theology. And in making the confession, he is worshiping God in his theology. It is a theology of worship and a theology of praise. His is making a statement about his beliefs in God.

Psalm 27 is a very personal statement and creed: the psalmist uses the word "my"—the Lord is *my* God. Of course we all know that God rules as the God of the universe, who is over everyone, but we must lay claim to him as our God. Every day we must confess that God is our God. Notice that the psalmist says, "my" light. This is not an abstract statement that indicates a vague belief in God. Even the Devil believes and trembles. No, David is not expressing a general belief. His belief is personal; his faith is real; and his theology is relational. The Lord is "my" God. He is a personal God. In Psalm 23, David declares, "The Lord is *my* shepherd, I shall not want. He makes *me* lie down in green pastures. He leads *me* beside the still waters. He restores *my* soul" (Psalm 23:1-3). If we could ever fully comprehend the depth of God's love and the personal nature of his relationship with us, it would transform our lives. God is a God who cares deeply for you and for me individually. God is not satisfied that we have a general belief in the existence of God, but he wants to be our covenant God. He wants to be our savior. He belongs to us and we belong to him. We have a very personal relationship with God. We are his "people and the sheep of his pasture" (Psalm 100:3). He has called us by name (Isaiah 43:1). We belong to him. We can trust him. We can trust him to be our life, our light, our salvation, our strength, our healer, our helper, and our song.

² When the wicked came against me to eat up my flesh,
My enemies and foes, they stumbled and fell.
³ Though an army may encamp against me,
My heart shall not fear;
Though war should rise against me,
I am trusting in this.

In verse two, the psalmist proclaims that he is trusting God to be his strength. He is trusting God to be his safety, even when he is surrounded. He is believing that God will be his security when the enemy comes against him.

Perhaps Peter was thinking of this verse when he wrote, "Satan, as a roaring lion, goes about seeking whom he may devour" (1 Peter 5:8). The enemy is seeking to devour us, to destroy us, to wipe us out. But the psalmist said, when the enemy, the wicked, came upon him to consume him, to devour him, they stumbled and fell. The enemy is pursuing us, but if we resist the Devil, he will flee from us. He will stumble and he will fall. Paul tells the Roman Christians, "The God of peace will soon crush Satan under your feet" (Romans 16:20).

In verse 3, the psalmist adds, "even though an army should encamp against me, my heart shall not fear, though war should rise against me, I am trusting in this." Even if we look out and there is an entire army surrounding us, God will protect us; he will make a way.

When the armies of the Assyrians surrounded Jerusalem, King Hezekiah went to the Lord in prayer, and God sent an angel to destroy the armies. Hezekiah admitted to God that the armies of the enemy were invincible and that he needed God's help. He prayed earnestly, "Save us; help us; deliver us". That night, the angel of the Lord came down into the camp of the Assyrians and killed 186,000 enemy soldiers. One angel is sufficient to destroy all the enemies that surround us. We read in Psalm 34:7 that the "angel of the Lord encamps around about those that fear him to deliver them." In the book of Revelation we see an angel with a chain in his hand who is coming down to bind the Devil and cast him into the bottomless pit. The Scripture says, "he laid hold of the dragon, that serpent of old, who is the Devil and Satan, and bound him" (Rev. 20:1). We think of the devil as a powerful enemy who has wrought havoc in the midst of the earth and against the church, but it requires only one angel to bind him and cast him into the bottomless pit.

When an army comes against us, God can deliver us. Sometimes we realize that our task is beyond our abilities, and the opposition is too strong. We may ask the question, "How can I overcome this? How can I get over this? How can I deal with this?" Perhaps our problems and troubles are so big that we completely lose hope. How can we deal with these impossible situations? How can we solve these problems? What can we do? The answer is to put our trust in the Lord. He is our light he is our salvation; he is our strength. He is the strength of those who trust in him.

God is a shelter for those who worship him.
One way that the Lord protects those who trust in him is to hide them in his shelter. He is a refuge to those that worship him. Verse four says,

⁴ One thing I have desired of the LORD, That will I seek:
    That I may dwell in the house of the LORD
    All the days of my life,
    To behold the beauty of the LORD,
    And to inquire in His temple.
⁵ For in the time of trouble
    He shall hide me in His pavilion;
    In the secret place of His tabernacle
        He shall hide me;
    He shall set me high upon a rock.
⁶ And now my head shall be lifted up
    above my enemies all around me;
    Therefore I will offer sacrifices of joy
        in His tabernacle;
    I will sing, yes, I will sing praises to the LORD.

The deepest desire of God's people is to dwell in the house of the Lord. The same sentiment is found in Psalm 23:6, where David announces, "I will dwell in the house of the Lord forever" and in Psalm 84, where we read,

¹ How lovely *is* Your tabernacle,
    O LORD of hosts!

² My soul longs, yes, even faints
    For the courts of the LORD; …
⁴ Blessed *are* those who dwell in Your house;
    They will still be praising You …
¹⁰ For a day in Your courts *is* better than a thousand.
    I would rather be a doorkeeper in the
        house of my God
    Than dwell in the tents of wickedness.

The Psalmist prays that he might dwell in the house of the Lord all the days of his life, to "behold the beauty of the Lord, and to inquire in his temple". His statement indicates that the worship of God is his greatest joy. To dwell in the house of the Lord means to remain there at all times. To behold the beauty of the Lord means to see God in all his glory. "Blessed are the pure in heart for they shall see God" (Matthew 5:8).

The one thing that David especially desires is to be in the house of God. It is there among the people of God that David can enjoy the Lord's presence, behold the Lord's beauty, and seek God's face. To be in the house of God is his constant passion, it is the goal and object of his life. Similarly, the early church exhibited a deep desire for constant worship and prayer. Luke reports that the early believers who were newly filled with the spirit continued "with one accord in the Temple" (Acts 2:46).

In his role as the King of Israel, David would have faced any number of daily challenges that would have occupied his time. Nevertheless, he chose to make attendance to the house of God one of his highest priorities. David's example should encourage us to evaluate our own priorities. In our technological age we are tempted to relegate the house of God to an afterthought while we are busy pursuing entertainment, pleasure, and affluence.

History teaches us that a passion for the house of God is a characteristic of revival and spiritual vitality. When God's people are spiritually alert, they never become weary of assembling together to worship the Lord. But when believers consider it a burden to attend to the services of worship, it is a clear sign of backsliding. David expresses his passionate desire for the presence of God not only here in Psalm 27, but also in Psalm Psalm 63:

¹ O God, thou art my God; early will I seek thee:
    my soul thirsteth for thee, my flesh longeth for thee
    in a dry and thirsty land, where no water is;
² To see thy power and thy glory,
    so as I have seen thee in the sanctuary.
³ Because thy lovingkindness is better than life,
    my lips shall praise thee.
⁴ Thus will I bless thee while I live:
    I will lift up my hands in thy name. (Psalm 63:1-4)

David's desire to be always in the house of God is, of course, not possible in this life. Therefore, if we are to be always in the presence of God, we must worship wherever we may find ourselves. We must "rejoice in the Lord always" (Philippians 4:4). Sometimes we think of worship as an activity that is confined going to church on Sunday, where we have praise and worship; we have a sermon; we may have prayer; then we go home. And we say we have worshiped. But for God's people worship is a way of life, and to dwell in the house of the Lord represents continual worship. We worship daily and continually. On Monday morning we arise and we make the house of the Lord our dwelling place. Our home should be the house of the Lord. When we drive our car, we should make it the house of the Lord, a place of worship. When we are on our jobs, we should make that place of sanctuary of God. Wherever we are we happen to be, we can lift our voices in praise to God. God wants to be present wherever we are. We must fellowship with him, commune with him, at all times. God wants to be present in our lives. We must practice the presence of God. For the Christian, God is always present. And we must live in light of the understanding that God is always with us. We are dwelling with God; we are beholding God; we're talking with God. This is our way of life. He is a refuge to those who worship him.

Those who worship him will enjoy special privileges—he will protect them in times of trouble. The psalmist says,

He shall hide me in His pavilion;
    In the secret place of His tabernacle
        He shall hide me;
    He shall set me high upon a rock (Psalm 27:5).

The psalmist is trusting in God's ability to hide him from all danger. The worshiper will be hidden in God's "pavilion", that is, his shelter. Also, he will be protected in the secret place of the tabernacle. If that is not sufficient protection, he will be set up high upon a rock. Why would he be placed upon a rock? Because a high rock is a place of safety, a place of security. Remember the words of Psalm 40:2, "he brought me up also out of a horrible pit, and he set my feet upon a rock, and established my going". He is a refuge for those who worship him.

God is the savior of those who call upon his name.
At this point in his experience, the psalmist is not facing any particular threat, but he prays that God will hear his cries for help should he ever find himself in trouble. Therefore, he asks the Lord saying,

⁷ Hear, O LORD, when I cry with my voice!
 Have mercy also upon me, and answer me.
⁸ When You said, "Seek My face,"
 My heart said to You, "Your face, LORD, I will seek."
⁹ Do not hide Your face from me;
 Do not turn Your servant away in anger;
 You have been my help;
 Do not leave me nor forsake me,
  O God of my salvation.
¹⁰ When my father and my mother forsake me,
 Then the LORD will take care of me.

First, the psalmist implores God for continuing mercy. Second, he promises to respond whenever God summons him to prayer. That is, his heart is always ready to seek God. Third, he pleads for God's ongoing presence in his life. Fourth, he affirms the Lord's tender care. Even when his father and mother would forsake him, the Lord will take him up. The Lord rescues those who call upon him.

When we get in trouble, we have several choices available to us. First, we can trust in our own resources and abilities to extract ourselves from trouble. Second, we can call on other people for help, a step that we should take more often in light of the Bible's exhortation that we confess our weaknesses one to another. We are encouraged to bear one another's burdens. But we can also take a third course of action—we can call upon the Lord.

The psalmist says, "Hear, O Lord ... do not hide your face." Have you ever prayed, but you felt like your prayers were not reaching God? Have you ever prayed, but you did not feel like God was listening? When we pray, we may not feel like God is listening, but we must trust that he is. We must come to God with an urgency in our prayers. There comes a time when we must persist in prayer, persevere in prayer.

There comes a time when we must be strong in our prayers, like the Canaanite woman who was following after Jesus. She cried continually, "Jesus, have mercy; my daughter is severely demon possessed" (Matthew 15:22-28). The disciples of Jesus commanded that she be quiet because she was a Gentile woman. They said, "Jesus came to minister to the Jews, not to the Gentiles." But Jesus asked her, "What do you want?" She replied, "I want my daughter to be healed." Jesus refused her plea, saying that he did not come to feed the dogs, but she responded to the rejection with the words, "Even the dogs eat the crumbs that fall from the master's table." At that point, Jesus said, "I have not seen such faith in all of Israel. Go your way; your daughter is healed." It is this kind of persistence that God wants to hear in our prayers; and when we cry out to him with passionate faith, he will hear us.

God is a steadfast guide for those who rely on him.
The psalmist maintains that even if his father and mother should forsake him, the Lord will continue to care for him. Furthermore, if his father and mother are not available to teach and guide him, he can depend upon the Lord to be his teacher and guide. The psalmist says,

[11] Teach me Your way, O LORD,
>   And lead me in a smooth path,
>   because of my enemies.
[12] Do not deliver me to the will of my adversaries;
>   For false witnesses have risen against me,
>   And such as breathe out violence.
[13] I would have lost heart, unless I had believed
>   That I would see the goodness of the LORD
>   In the land of the living.

¹⁴ Wait on the LORD; Be of good courage,
   And He shall strengthen your heart;
   Wait, I say, on the LORD!

The psalmist trusts that God will be his guide. He prays, "Teach me your way, O Lord". God's ways are not our ways. We have our own ways. We have our own plans. We have our own schemes and ideas. David, however, prays, "Teach me *your* way, O Lord".

Whenever we have choices to make, we may weigh the pros and cons of each option that is available to us. But we do not know the future, and we do not have wisdom equal to the wisdom of God. We do not know all of the aspects of a problem like God knows them.

We need to realize that when we trust in the Lord, he will lead us in the right way—his way, not our way. He will lead us in the way that he wants us to go. He knows what is best for us, and he knows the future. He knows the way that we should go. He knows the path that we need to take.

If we will trust in him, God will lead us. However, he does not always answer us as quickly as we would like. The psalmist, therefore, encourages us to "wait upon the Lord and be of good courage." Waiting upon the Lord is difficult for us. We can grow quite impatient. We want to know the answers, and we want to know them now. Waiting is not something that we like to do, but we need to come to the place where we can trust God and say, "Lord, my life is in your hands. My future is in your hands; my way is in your hands. And Lord God, I am waiting upon you, and I am trusting in you."

This Psalm teaches us to put our trust and faith in God. In the last verse, David tells us to "wait on the Lord and be of good courage." He means that we are to wait in faith not in doubt. That is why he said, "be of good courage." We wait with confidence; we wait with hope; we wait with trust; we wait with belief, with faith, not in fear. There is an old story that my mother told me when I was a boy—it is called "Chicken Little". Chicken Little ran from one person to another crying out, "The sky is falling; the sky is falling." We must not take on the attitude of Chicken Little while we're waiting on God. Any suspicions that the sky is falling are counterproductive to our faith and to our prayers. We wait upon

God in full anticipation that he will hear our prayers and he will provide for us the guidance that we need. We may not know what he will do, but we know he will act, and he will act powerfully. He will do something. We would do well to remember the promise of Isaiah chapter 40:31, which says, "They that wait upon the Lord shall renew their strength. They shall mount up with wings like an eagle. They shall run and not be weary; they shall walk and not faint". Wait upon the Lord. The Lord is our light, the Lord is our salvation, the Lord is the strength of our life, when we are in trouble, and when we are in need, and when we are in distress, we must wait upon him, and trust in the Lord. He is our guide, and we can trust in him.

The Lord is watching over us. In Luke 12, Jesus said that God sees every sparrow that falls, and how much more does God care for us than for the sparrows. And he said that everything we do, God sees it. Every thought that we think, God knows it. God has numbered the hairs of our heads. God understands and knows exactly who we are, where we are, and where we need to be going with our lives. With David we say, "Wait on the Lord and be of good courage, and he will strengthen your heart."

Conclusion

One of the most beloved types of psalms is the Psalm of Trust. Psalm 23 is a Psalm of Trust: "The Lord is my shepherd I will not want". The Psalm of Trust is an expression of faith and trust that God is with his people and that God is their helper. The psalm that we just studied, Psalm 27, is also a psalm of trust. It begins with the words,

> The Lord is my light and my salvation. Whom shall I fear? The Lord is the strength of my life. Of whom shall I be afraid? When my enemies and foes came against me to eat up my flesh, they stumbled and fell. Though a host would encamp against me, in this I will be confident (Ps. 27.1-3).

Our faith is fundamental to our relationship with God. But sometimes, we are be tempted to think of faith only as the ability to do something great—to do a miracle, to move mountains, to accomplish something spectacular. But there is a certain kind of faith in the Bible that is exemplified in Psalm 27, it is the faith of constant trust, the faith in God that stands fast when we are under attack from the enemy. When we are surrounded, we say, "I will believe the Lord no matter what is happening. I will trust God." It is a kind of constancy, a kind of firmness, a kind of steadfastness. And it is like what Paul is talking about when he says to the Corinthians, "Be steadfast, immovable, always abounding in the work of the Lord, knowing that your labor is not in vain in the Lord" (1 Corinthians 15:58). It is the kind of trust that exemplified in his own life when he says,

> We are troubled on every side but not distressed,
> perplexed but not in despair,
> persecuted but not forsaken,
> cast down but not destroyed (2 Corinthians 4:8-9).

How can we maintain this level of hope? Because we are trusting in the Lord. This kind of trust is what the writer of Hebrews 11 is talking about when he says,

> By faith Abel offered up to God a more excellent sacrifice than Cain … By faith Noah built the ark, and he saved his family … By faith Abraham went out to the land that God gave him, even though he did not know where he was going … By faith Moses left Egypt and chose to be with God's people rather than to enjoy the pleasures of sin temporarily … By faith the walls of Jericho fell down.

These were people who trusted God in the midst of difficult circumstances and in the midst of challenging times. They were not always appreciated, applauded, or supported by their contemporaries. More often, they were ridiculed, persecuted, and judged to be mentally unstable.

We are living in perilous times, but it is in these times that we should trust God and believe that he will do something great through us. It is when our society is in deep trouble that we as Christians must stand up in faith and demonstrate that we trust God. We will be like a light on the hilltop, like a candle in the darkness. Let us be a witness to God's goodness.

We may want to offer a prayer like this:

Oh Lord, we bow before you in humility, yet in confidence. Our confidence rests in your grace and in your goodness. You have promised to be our guide, and we come to you now, asking for that guidance that only you can give. You are our teacher, and we confess that we need to learn from you. We need to trust in you and rely upon you. Oh Lord, help me to stop doubting your love and resisting your grace. I praise you, I worship you, I glorify you. Let me stand fast through the difficult times. And let my life be a witness to everyone who is around me. Oh Lord, you are my light; you are my salvation; you are the strength of my life. I will not be afraid. When the enemy comes against me he will stumble and fall. We will dwell in your house. We will worship you. We will glorify you. Hallelujah!

❧ **Chapter 5** ❧

Sharing a Thankful Testimony

Psalm 30
A Psalm. A Song at the dedication of the house of David.
¹ I will extol You, O LORD, for You have lifted me up,
     And have not let my foes rejoice over me.
² O LORD my God, I cried out to You,
     And You healed me.
³ O LORD, You brought my soul up from the grave;
     You have kept me alive,
     that I should not go down to the pit.
⁴ Sing praise to the LORD, You saints of His,
     And give thanks at the remembrance of
     His holy name.
⁵ For His anger is but for a moment,
     His favor is for life;
     Weeping may endure for a night,
     But joy comes in the morning.
⁶ Now in my prosperity I said,
     "I shall never be moved."
⁷ LORD, by Your favor
     You have made my mountain stand strong;
     You hid Your face, and I was troubled.
⁸ I cried out to You, O LORD;
     And to the LORD I made supplication:
⁹ "What profit is there in my blood,
     When I go down to the pit? Will the dust praise You?
     Will it declare Your truth?
¹⁰ Hear, O LORD, and have mercy on me;

LORD, be my helper!"
¹¹ You have turned for me my mourning into dancing;
   You have put off my sackcloth
   and clothed me with gladness,
¹² To the end that my glory may sing praise to You
   and not be silent.
   O LORD my God, I will give thanks to You forever.

The Gospel of Luke tells the story of ten desperate lepers who sought for Jesus and his healing touch. As Jesus entered their village, they stood at a distance, afraid to approach him because their leprousy made them "untouchable".

And they lifted up their voices and said, "Jesus, Master, have mercy on us!" So when He saw them, He said to them, "Go, show yourselves to the priests." And so it was that as they went, they were cleansed. And one of them, when he saw that he was healed, returned, and with a loud voice glorified God, and fell down on his face at His feet, giving Him thanks. And he was a Samaritan. So Jesus answered and said, "Were there not ten cleansed? But where are the nine? "Were there not any found who returned to give glory to God except this foreigner?" And He said to him, "Arise, go your way. Your faith has made you well." (Luke 17:12-19)

The story of the ten lepers teaches the value of giving thanks to God. When God does something for us, we should thank him. When God hears our cries and does a mighty work in our lives, we must not simply go on our way. But we must stop what we're doing and return to give thanks to God for his mercy and grace. All of the 10 lepers were healed, but only one returned to give thanks. The other nine went on about their business. The one leper praised and glorified God with a "loud voice". He was not ashamed for other people to hear what had happened. He did not go back and whisper it to Jesus, but he spoke it loudly. Like this leper who fell down at the feet of Jesus, we should be praising God at every opportunity. We can never praise God too much. Paul encouraged us saying, "in everything give thanks, for this is the will of God in Christ Jesus concerning you" (1 Thess. 5:18 KJV). Like Paul, the Psalmist teaches us the value of constant praise. At all times we should be giving thanks to God. Psalm 30 tells us that we should worship God with our thankful testimony; that is, we should praise God with a testimony of what the Lord has done for us.

Psalm 30: Worship through Thankful Testimony

As we look at this Psalm, there are two things that we should notice. First, we should notice how the Lord appears near the first of many of the verses. This Psalm is directed toward the Lord. The psalmist puts the Lord up front in his praise. In our testimonies, God should claim priority. We may be tempted to praise ourselves as much or more than we praise God. Our praise should be directed to god. We should say, "You healed me. You brought me up. You turned my mourning into dancing. You clothed me with joy. You kept me alive." Our praise needs to be offered directly to God.

But suddenly in v. 4, after praising God directly, the psalmist changes direction and begins speaking to the people. He invites the congregation: "Sing praise to the Lord." He encourages them to praise God along with him. His invitation reminds me of another psalm where he sings, "O magnify the Lord with me, and let us exalt his name together" (Ps. 34:3).

The Title of Psalm 30

A Psalm. A Song at the dedication of the house of David.

The title of this Psalm is "A Psalm. A Song at the dedication of the house of David". The house would be the palace of David which he built near the end of his life. It would not be the Temple, because Solomon, David's son, built the temple. David desired to build the Temple, but God would not allow him to do so. David prayed and said, "Lord, I have built a beautiful new house, and now I would like to build a house for you." But the Lord said, "it is not for you to build my house, because you have been a man of war; your son will build my house". And then God added, "but I will build your house" (2 Samuel 7). The word "house" refers to David's household, his royal dynasty. God goes on to say that a son of David will always be upon the throne of Israel.

The psalmist will praise God

¹ I will extol You, O LORD, for You have lifted me up,
      And have not let my foes rejoice over me.
² O LORD my God, I cried out to You,
      And You healed me.
³ O LORD, You brought my soul up from the grave;
      You have kept me alive,
      that I should not go down to the pit.

In verse one, the song starts out with the words, "I will extol you, O Lord." The word "extol" means to raise up high; therefore, in the context of worship, extol means to exalt, magnify, to lift up God's name. Why should we extol God? We lift him up because he has lifted us up. The Hebrew word that is translated "lifted up" means to pull up, such as pulling up of a water bucket out of the well. Therefore, we lift him up because he has reached down and pulled us up. It reminds me of Psalm 40 where David said, "he pulled me up out of a horrible pit, out of the miry clay, and he set my feet upon a rock" (v. 2). We were in the pit, but he lifted us up, and because he lifted us up, we will raise him up. We will lift him up in praise. Here in Psalm 30, he praises God for keeping him free of the pit: "you preserved my life that I should not go down into the pit" (v. 3).

David also praised God because when he cried out to God, he healed him. The word "cried" is not the usual Hebrew expression for calling upon God. There are two words that are used commonly in the Old Testament. The word *qara* means to cry out in the sense of making noise, an audible utterance. It is also used of reading aloud such as reading a letter, and it is used of greeting someone, calling out, "Hello". Another word that means to cry out is *tsaaq*, which signifies calling out for help. The word used here is neither of those, instead the word here means to scream over and over, to cry out loudly and continually. David is saying, "Oh Lord, I was screaming out for help to you, and you healed me".

Then the psalmist expands his reason for praise. He says, "You brought up my soul from the grave, you kept me alive that I should not go down into the pit". It says literally, "you preserved my life from the pit". Our lives are in the hands of God; he preserves us from death. Therefore, let us praise him.

The congregation is invited to join in the praise

⁴ Sing praise to the LORD, You saints of His,
      And give thanks at the remembrance of
      His holy name.
⁵ For His anger is but for a moment,
      His favor is for life;
      Weeping may endure for a night,
      But joy comes in the morning.

Next, the psalmist speaks to the congregation, summoning them to join him in worship. He invites them, "Sing praise to the Lord". The Hebrew word "sing" refers to playing a musical instrument, plucking the strings. A better translation would be, "make music unto the Lord". The Lord loves music. He never tires of listening to our music when it's offered in praise to him. Pentecostals have always been known for their music, and we should continue to be known for our music. Our churches should be filled with music of praise: the sound of the piano, the keyboard, the organ, trumpet, drums, the guitar, and every other kind of instrument. God loves music. Make music to the Lord!

He says, make music to the Lord, you saints. The word "saints" here is also unusual. The common word for saint is *qadosh*, which means holy one. But the word used here is *hasid*, meaning faithful one. *Hasid* comes from the Hebrew word *hesed*, which signifies covenant faithfulness. The ultra-conservative Jewish group known as the Hasidim (or Hasidic Jews) derive their name from *hasid*. The psalmist, therefore, is inviting everyone who is faithful to the cove-nant to praise God. He is saying, "Everyone who is faithful, come and praise God. Make music to the Lord, faithful people". God's faithful followers should sing praise, make music, and give thanks. Giving thanks signifies testifying publicly, giving a praise testimony.

This worship in music and praise should take place "at the re-membrance of his Holiness". Whenever we remember that God is holy, we should praise him. What does it mean when we say that God is holy? It means that God always acts in accordance with his character of justice and love. That is, God's nature is consistent. He is a God of integrity. His nature is righteous, good, and just. Every-thing that God does flows out of his love and his righteousness.

Yes, God does get angry, but he never gets angry without good reason, and his anger is always momentary. The Hebrew says literally, "his anger is a moment". His anger always justified and it is manifested only in redemptive ways. It is intended to produce human change for the good.

God's anger is momentary, but "his favor is for life" (v. 5). The King James uses the word "favor", but a better translation is "pleasure". Therefore, the psalmist is saying that God is only angry with us for a moment, but he takes pleasure in us all of our life. God takes pleasure in his people forever. He looks upon us with great pleasure, and that is a wonderful thing. It is very much the way that we look upon our children—with joy. When we think of our children it brings great pleasure to our hearts. We are well aware that our children will do things that we do not approve of, and they will at times disappoint us. Sometimes we are even angry at our children. But our anger is temporary. Our pleasure in them lasts all the days of their lives.

God's anger does not last and neither does our sorrow— "Weeping may endure for a night, but joy comes in the morning". The words, "endure for a night", mean literally to take lodging overnight. That is, weeping is only a temporary guest, like a guest in a motel who stays only for the night. Weeping will come in and take the spare bed, and stay for the night, but joy (literally "the shout") will come in the morning. Even if we sleep with weeping we can wake up with shouting. The Psalm is telling us of the temporary nature of sorrow and pain. God's people certainly face troubles, but troubles do not last. The joy of the Lord lasts forever. Many afflictions come to righteous people, but "the Lord delivers them from them all" (Ps. 34:8). When we are going through a time of trouble, we think the pain will never end, but it will. One night of suffering can seem like an eternity, but joy comes in the morning.

The psalmist shares his testimony

> [6] Now in my prosperity I said,
>   "I shall never be moved."
> [7] LORD, by Your favor
>   You have made my mountain stand strong;
>   You hid Your face, and I was troubled.
> [8] I cried out to You, O LORD;

And to the LORD I made supplication:
9 "What profit is there in my blood,
    When I go down to the pit? Will the dust praise You?
    Will it declare Your truth?
10 Hear, O LORD, and have mercy on me;
    LORD, be my helper!"
11 You have turned for me my mourning into dancing;
    You have put off my sackcloth
    and clothed me with gladness,
12 To the end that my glory may sing praise to You
    and not be silent.
    O LORD my God, I will give thanks to You forever.

His distress

Next, the psalmist goes back and recounts his trouble. He says, "in my prosperity (a time of quietness or ease, when everything was going well) I said, 'I will never be moved' (shaken). He believed that everything was going right, and he would never be shaken. He continued, "Lord, … you hid your face, and I was troubled (disturbed).

His cry for help

He says, "I cried out to you, Lord". The word "cried" is *tsaaq*, the usual word for crying out for help. In addition to crying out, he "made supplication", which means to seek for God's favor, to seek for God's grace. He was in need, and he cried out to the Lord, and he gives the content of his prayer. He tells us exactly what he prayed. In his prayer, he asked, "What profit (gain) is there in my blood, when I go down to the pit? Will the dust praise you? Will it declare your truth?" (v. 9) Will the dust offer testimony to God's goodness? He reasons that if he dies, his testimony will be silenced. He also pleaded with God: "Hear, O Lord and have mercy (show favor, grace) on me. Lord, be my helper." He prayed for God's mercy, grace, and help.

His deliverance

God answered David's prayer. The answer is stated here in figurative terms. The psalmist shouts, "You have turned my mourning into dancing" (v. 11). Here is the answer. The word "mourning" means literally "wailing". But God has answered and turned his wailing into dancing. It was common in biblical times for mourners to wail and scream out in anguish. They would even hire mourners at times in order to make a greater impact. The mourning garments of sackcloth have been replaced with "gladness". Joy has returned to his house.

His promise to continue praising God

The psalmist declares that God's act of deliverance has a purpose. God answered his prayers so that he might "sing praise" to God, that he might make music to the Lord and "not be silent" (v. 12). In one final burst of gratitude, he proclams, "O Lord my God, I will give thanks to you forever". The word "thanks" is *yadah*, which means the offering of a thankful testimony of praise for this specific divine intervention. Psalm 30 therefore, begins with praise, "I will extol you Lord", and it ends with praise, "I will continue to praise you". We can never praise God too much. Let us begin our days with praise, and let us end our days with praise. Let us praise him! God is listening for our cries. Let us pray in times of need and let us praise him when he answers. God is interested in our lives; he is interested in what is happening. We cannot see him; but he is here. We know this by faith. If we listen to the voices around us in the world, we would come to the conclusion that God does not exist or that God does not care and that we are all alone. But Jesus said, "I will never leave you and I will never forsake you" (Heb. 13:5). Therefore, let us pray, and let us praise.

Songs of Praise

There are two kinds of praise psalms in the book of Psalms. One type of praise Psalm, exemplified by Psalm 30, is a psalm that praises God for a specific act that God has done. We call this a Psalm of thankful testimony. The second type of praise Psalm is called the hymn. The hymn praises God not for one specific answer to prayer or deliverance but for God's nature and character. We will take a look at the hymns in a later chapter.

This particular type of Psalm, the Psalm of thankful testimony, sometimes called the thanksgiving Psalm, records the praises of an individual who comes back to God and says to God, "Lord, I was in trouble and you helped me, I was lost and you found me, I was in need and you supplied that need. You delivered me, you came to my rescue, and now I want to praise you for your answer, for your help, for your deliverance". Again, a Psalm of thankful testimony is a praise Psalm that gives thanks to God for a specific action in the life of an individual or of the congregation.

Genuine praise flows out of deep prayer

The psalms of thankful praise are related to the psalms of urgent prayer that we studied earlier. More specifically, the relationship between prayer psalms and praise Psalms shows that praise is a product of prayer. Psalms 13 and 22 were both prayers that were uttered by the psalmist in the midst of trouble, from the pit of despair. In these prayers psalmist brings his need before God. He prays, "How long, O Lord, will you forget me?" (Ps. 13:1) He cries out, "My God, my God, why have you forsaken me?" (Ps. 22:1) In the prayer psalms, the psalmist describes an urgent need and calls upon God's assistance. The painful experience of the psalmist is expressed in the form of a petition to God. In one case he prays, "O Lord my God, save me" (Ps. 7:1). But within that same Psalm, there is a promise of praise. He says, "I will praise the Lord according to his righteousness, and I will sing praise the name of the Lord most high" (Ps. 7:17). The psalmist promises that whenever God answers, he will praise God.

That promise of praise is very important. What God wants from us more than anything else is our love and devotion. If he has our heart then he has all of us. Jesus said, "you shall love the Lord your God with all your heart"; this is the greatest commandment (Matt. 22:37-38). As Christians, it is our desire to live a life that pleases God. Thus, we try to do things that will make God pleased with us. However, in all of our activity, doing things for God, let us not forget to express our praise, thanksgiving, and affection for God. As we walk in relationship with God, we must remember that God appreciates a grateful heart. He appreciates our worship of him and the giving of ourselves to him as a living sacrifice (Rom. 12:1).

Prayer precedes praise

So, first comes the prayer—
  "How long, O Lord" (Ps. 13:1).
Then comes the praise—
  "I will sing unto the Lord" (Ps. 13:6).

Likewise, Psalm 22 begins with prayer—

"My God, my God, why have you forsaken me?" (v. 1)

Afterwards, comes a promise of praise—

"My praise shall be of you in the great assembly" (v. 25).

Notice the future tense used by the Psalmist: "I will praise you"; "I will give you thanks"; "I will sing praises".

The vow of praise

Finally, near the end of Psalm 22, he declares, "I will pay my vows". The vow is a promise to offer up a sacrifice, a thanksgiving offering, a sacrifice in the Temple. So, the Psalms of prayer include a promise to praise God. The psalmist declares, "my praise shall be of you in the great assembly. I will pay my vows for those who fear him" (v. 25). The recital of the psalm of thanksgiving is a part of the psalmist's fulfillment of his promise to praise God. The person who prays the urgent prayer of lament puts it in the form of a Psalm, in that psalm includes a promise to praise God once he answers the prayer. Then, when the answer comes, the person who prayed will compose a Psalm of praise in fulfillment of their promise. Therefore, the psalm of urgent prayer is followed by the psalm of thankful testimony.

The praise and thanksgiving issues forth from the heart of prayer. What is wrong with a lot of praise is that it does not come forth from a prayerful life. In order to praise God fully, we must first spend time in the presence of God prayerfully submitting ourselves to God, seeking the face of God. We must first surrender to God, bring our needs before God, and turn them over to God. We cannot ignore God throughout the week and then walk into God's house on Sunday with the expectation that he will pour out his Spirit upon us and bless our praises. Without prayer, our praises are shallow and empty. Deep and heartfelt prayer always precedes Pentecost. Glorious times of praise and worship are always built upon the foundation of prayer and fasting. We must open ourselves up and pour ourselves out to God before he will pour out his Spirit upon us. The greatest praise comes after we have taken time to really seek God with all our heart. When we have sought God diligently and urgently and God has answered our prayers and delivered us from the enemy, then praise will come easily from our lips. No one will have to beg us to worship. The pastor would not have to prompt us to praise God. The worship leader will find it easy to lead, because we will be ready to praise God.

The thanksgiving sacrifice

The psalm of thanksgiving is the fulfillment of the promise to praise God. Further, the vow refers to a thanksgiving offering. The person whose prayer God had answered would bring an offering, a sacrifice, to the Temple as a sacrifice of praise. This thanksgiving sacrifice would vary according to the financial abilities of the giver. The animal would be brought to the temple and handed over to the priest, who would slaughter the animal. The skin of the animal, along with its insides, would be burned on the altar. The edible parts of the animal, the meat, would be cooked in a pot of boiling water. Once the meat had finished cooking, the priest would take a large fork and stick it down into the meat. Whatever portion was retrieved with the fork belonged to the priest. The remainder of the cooked meat would form the basis of a fellowship meal for the person who made the sacrifice and for his family and friends. During this fellowship meal, which we could also call a thanksgiving meal, the person who offered the sacrifice would share a testimony of God's gracious work in his or her life. They would tell the story of their time of trouble, their prayer, and God's deliverance. Everyone would celebrate what God had done in the life of the believer. And they would sing songs of testimony and praise. In the book of Leviticus, when it talks about the offerings, it says that if the sacrifice is in fulfillment of a vow, it should be eaten on the same day that the sacrifice was made. They would eat it either at or near the Temple in celebration of the testimony of the person who had been delivered by the power of God.

The testimony was given publicly to the family, friends, and the congregation that had gathered. We often overlook the fact that in the Bible, the word "thanksgiving" does not refer to a private attitude of gratefulness. The giving of thanks is not a private matter, it is a public display of testimony and witness to God's work. It is a public, outward testimony to the congregation of what God has done. The biblical concept of thanksgiving always involves public testimony of praise.

Structure of the Psalms of Thanksgiving

These thanksgiving psalms, although they vary in form, will normally have three parts. First is the introduction; second is a narration of the divine intervention; and third is the conclusion. In the introduction, the psalmist will declare his or her intention to praise the Lord: "I will praise the Lord". The psalmist will then give a general reason for praising the Lord. The second part of the psalm, the narration, looks back and recounts the events of being in trouble, the prayer to God, and God's intervention. The third part of the psalm, the conclusion, restates the psalmist's intent to praise God, and it will offer descriptive praise to God. Descriptive praise is praise for God's character and his nature, a statement of God's goodness. For example, "The Lord is great and greatly to be praised". Descriptive praise does not mention a specific event; instead, it declares God's positive attributes.

We can outline the psalms of thanksgiving as follows (references to Psalm 30 are in parentheses):

I. Introduction
    A. Intent to Praise God (v. 1a)
    B. Summary of Why (v. 1b-3)
II. Narration of the Divine Intervention
    A. Distress (vv. 6-7)
    B. Cry for Help (vv. 8-10)
    C. Deliverance (v. 11)
III. Conclusion
    A. Renewed Vow of Praise (v. 12)
    B. Descriptive Praise (vv. 4-5)

Let us this structure to Psalm 30. The psalmist starts out with the intent to praise God: "I will extol you Lord". This is the beginning of the Psalm. Then he gives a reason for praise: "because you have lifted me up, and you have not let my enemies rejoice over me. Oh Lord, I cried to you for help and you healed me ". That is the reason for praise. That is why he's praising God. Next comes the narration, in which the psalmist tells in more detail what happened. This second part of the Thanksgiving Psalm tells about the specific events surrounding the psalmist's need, prayer, and God's answer.

"In my prosperity I said, I will never be moved, and you hid your face from me, and I was dismayed". His trouble is summarized in terms of God's absence, which resulted in the psalmist's feelings of dismay. Next, he relates that he sought God in prayer: "but to you O Lord, I cried, and I made supplication". He looks back to his time of prayer and restates the words that he uttered to God. Next, he tells about his deliverance. "I was in trouble, I cried out, but you have turned my mourning into dancing".

The truth is that many Christians practice neither prevailing prayer nor passionate praise. It is not that we lack occasions for urgent prayer. We do have those occasions: times of suffering, times of pain, times of grief and sorrow. However, when we encounter pressure, pain, and suffering, we are tempted to pursue one of two unhelpful options. First, we may give up, resigning ourselves to a life of suffering. If we do not believe that God is genuinely involved in our lives and that he will intervene, then prayer is essentially a ritual that accomplishes little. Do we really believe that God answers prayer? The second unhelpful option is the positive confession approach. We could also call this the "denial of reality" approach. Some well-meaning faith teachers have told us that we should never speak any negative words. We should never confess that we are weak, that we are sick, that we have doubts, or that we are struggling in any way. They say that we should only speak words of victory, conquest, prosperity, health, wealth, joy, rejoicing, and happiness. Such an approach, however, is not biblical. Instead of denying that we are weak, the Bible teaches us to admit our weaknesses. Instead of denying that we are sick, the Bible tells us to call upon other believers to pray for us that we may be healed. As we mentioned earlier, the psalms of urgent prayer, in which sin is confessed and pain is expressed, are the most common type of psalm in the book of Psalms.

It also is not the case that we lack occasions to utter exuberant praise. The many times that God intervenes in our lives are just such occasions. He answers our prayers, so let us praise him. He heals our sicknesses, so let us praise him. He blesses our children, so let us praise him. He delivers us from danger, so let us praise him. In our culture, exuberant and passionate emotion is commonly limited to the rock concert and the sports stadium. If we can be enthusiastic about the transitory and ultimately insignificant results of sports contest, then why can we not become enthusiastic in our worship of the God of the universe, creator of all things, the sustainer of life, the King of kings, and the Lord of lords who is coming to rule and reign over the earth in his eternal kingdom?

In times of pain, we ought to be praying, and in times of joy, we ought to be shouting. The psalmist says, "he has replaced my sackcloth with gladness" (30:11). What is sackcloth? It is the cheap and rough cloth that was worn in ancient times as a sign of mourning. Its significance is similar to the more recent practice of wearing black. The removal of sackcloth is a symbolic way of saying to God, "you have removed my grief". The Psalms are written in poetic form and they use figurative, vivid language to go beyond the simple statement of deliverance. Mourning is turned into dancing and sackcloth is turned into gladness. The language is moving and exciting.

The psalm ends with a renewed vow of praise: "Oh Lord God, I will give thanks to you for ever". In many cases, the psalms of thanksgiving conclude with a verse of descriptive praise. But in this particular case, the descriptive praise is not at the end of the Psalm; it is in the middle. The psalmist had the liberty of moving things around a bit. The outline of the Psalms is not static but is dynamic. The descriptive praise is found in vv. 4-5: "Sing praise to the Lord, you his saints; give thanks to his holy name, for his anger is momentary, but his favor is lifelong". He is calling on the congregation to give praise along with him. He exhorts the believers to praise God because of God's nature and character. The specific attribute that the psalmist points to is God's grace, his favor. The anger of God is temporary, but the grace of God is forever. Humans sometimes provoke God's anger, but his anger does not last. Anger is not a part of the nature of God, rather, it is a response to human sin and disobedience. The anger of God only lasts for a short time. But his grace, his favor, endures throughout our lives. His favor never expires; it never runs out; it is never depleted; and it is never insufficient.

Conclusion

The Song of Testimony, or Thanksgiving Psalm, is a public celebration of answered prayer. It is a public testimonial to all who are present that God has intervened in the life of the worshiper. The thanksgiving psalm is based upon the final element of the lament. At the end of the lament, the petitioner promises that when the prayer has been answered, he or she will offer a thanksgiving sacrifice. After God has answered the prayer and brought deliverance, the psalmist comes with his or her family and friends to the temple. At the temple, an offering or sacrifice is made in thanks to God. A Song of Testimony is sung to commemorate the occasion in praise to God.

The Song of Testimony teaches us the value of public thanksgiving. This kind of psalm is meant to encourage the congregation who hear the song. Our deliverance is not complete until we give witness to it. God's purposes in bringing deliverance are incomplete without our testimony. The Song of Testimony teaches us the value of sharing our personal experiences with others. Our children need to hear that God has answered our prayers. Our friends and family need to hear what God has done in our lives. Some churches have become very impersonal, and the members of the congregation no longer share their lives with each other. These psalms demonstrate the value of telling our story to one another in the context of worship.

The Songs of Testimony include Psalms 30, 34, 41, 66, 84, 87, 91, 92, 103, 111, 116, 118, 121, 122, 131, 138, 139, and 146.

Chapter 6

Victory in Times of Reversal

Psalm 40
To the Chief Musician. A Psalm of David.
[1] I waited patiently for the LORD;
    And He inclined to me, And heard my cry.
[2] He also brought me up out of a horrible pit,
    Out of the miry clay,
    And set my feet upon a rock,
    And established my steps.
[3] He has put a new song in my mouth—
    Praise to our God;
    Many will see it and fear, And will trust in the LORD.
[4] Blessed is that man who makes the LORD his trust,
    And does not respect the proud,
    nor such as turn aside to lies.
[5] Many, O LORD my God, are Your wonderful works
    Which You have done;
    And Your thoughts toward us
    Cannot be recounted to You in order;
    If I would declare and speak of them,
    They are more than can be numbered.
[6] Sacrifice and offering You did not desire;
    My ears You have opened.
    Burnt offering and sin offering You did not require.
[7] Then I said, "Behold, I come;
    In the scroll of the book it is written of me.
[8] I delight to do Your will, O my God,
    And Your law is within my heart."

⁹ I have proclaimed the good news of righteousness
>   In the great assembly;
>   Indeed, I do not restrain my lips,
>   O LORD, You Yourself know.
¹⁰ I have not hidden Your righteousness within my heart;
>   I have declared Your faithfulness and Your salvation;
>   I have not concealed Your lovingkindness
>   and Your truth
>   From the great assembly.
¹¹ Do not withhold Your tender mercies from me,
>   O LORD;
>   Let Your lovingkindness and Your truth
>   continually preserve me.
¹² For innumerable evils have surrounded me;
>   My iniquities have overtaken me,
>   so that I am not able to look up;
>   They are more than the hairs of my head;
>   Therefore my heart fails me.
¹³ Be pleased, O LORD, to deliver me;
>   O LORD, make haste to help me!
¹⁴ Let them be ashamed and brought to mutual confusion
>   Who seek to destroy my life;
>   Let them be driven backward
>   and brought to dishonor
>   Who wish me evil.
¹⁵ Let them be confounded because of their shame,
>   Who say to me, "Aha, aha!"
¹⁶ Let all those who seek You rejoice and be glad in You;
>   Let such as love Your salvation say continually,
>   "The LORD be magnified!"
¹⁷ But I am poor and needy;
>   Yet the LORD thinks upon me.
>   You are my help and my deliverer;
>   Do not delay, O my God.

Has anybody ever said to you, "I have good news and I have bad news. Which do you want first?" Psalm 40 is a bit like that. It starts with the good news and then moves on to the bad news. Unfortunately, the Psalm reflects the realities of life. Sometimes we hardly have time to enjoy a blessing from God before we are blindsided by another attack of the enemy. We have trials and tribulations, and we pray, and we ask for God's help. Then we are overjoyed when God delivers us. But just as soon as he delivers us from one trouble, our rejoicing is interrupted by another test. I have witnessed the despair brought on by these kinds of experiences. I've heard friends say, "I just recovered from one problem, and now I'm facing another problem". An old saying is "when it rains it pours". Did you ever feel like you're gone as far as you could go? Does it seem that you are at the end of your rope?

The early Christians faced a situation like this. On the day of Pentecost the Holy Spirit is poured out, and the believers rejoice in their newfound blessing. Peter preaches to the crowd and 3000 people are converted. The apostles are filled with joy and with expectation for the days of revival that lie ahead. Miracles are happening. In Acts 3, Peter and John encounter a lame man, and God heals him. Peter says, "I have no silver; and I have no gold; what I have I give to you. In the name of Jesus Christ of Nazareth, rise up and walk". Peter reached down and took the lame man by the hand and lifted him up. They are rejoicing in the healing of the lame man, and in the conversion of large numbers of people. But they had little time to enjoy these blessings. Very quickly they were arrested and thrown into jail, and the authorities ordered them to stop preaching in the name of Jesus. They were accused of stirring up trouble. Thus, they are rejoicing one day and they are in prison the next day. Sometimes that is the way it happens. I wonder if you have experienced a similar pattern? You were in trouble and prayed earnestly, and God answered. So you were shouting the victory, but suddenly you are struck with another problem.

We looked at both Psalm 13 and Psalm 22, both of which are fervent, passionate pleas for God's help. They are called psalms of lament. We called them psalms of urgent prayer. They are expressions of prayer in the time of trouble. Then, we looked at Psalm 30, which is a psalm of thankful testimony, a psalm that is sung by someone who has come out of trouble—someone who prayed the prayer of faith, and God brought an answer. In the previous chapter, we talked about the fact that the greatest praise flows out of deep prayers of lament. It is in the valley that God restores our soul. When we are coming out of a deep trial, the praise is wonderful because it bursts forth from our innermost being. In those times we do not praise God because we ought to, but we praise God because we want to. The praise flows freely from within.

It is normal for praise to follow closely upon a time of sincere prayer, as in the psalms of urgent prayer. But life is not always predictable. Instead of beginning with prayer and concluding with praise, Psalm 40 begins as a psalm of thanksgiving, but ends with a plea for help. This psalm shows us that we can be in the midst of praising God, when all of a sudden, we find the need to pray because tragedy or disaster has struck. The psalmist is at first praising God for how God delivered him in the past, but then he sees that he is in trouble again, and he needs God's help.

This psalm takes us on an emotional roller coaster. It begins with the joy of deliverance and ends with a plea for new deliverance:

1. Deliverance and Joy (vv. 1-3)
2. God's wonderful works (vv. 4-5)
3. Gratitude and offering (vv. 6-8)
4. Testifying of God's faithfulness (vv. 9-10)
5. A new threat (vv. 11-12)
6. Prayer for help (vv. 13-17)

The psalmist start out praising God for deliverance, then he must face new disaster that strikes. The psalm is true to life, sometimes our day starts out high, then things go down. We must face these kind of days with faith in the Lord, with trust in God. The first part of the psalm, verses one through three, speaks of deliverance and joy. Then, in verses four and five, he talks about God's wonderful works. In verses six through eight, he talks about being grateful and bringing an offering. But God doesn't really want an offering—God wants his praise—so in verses nine and 10, the psalmist is praising God, testifying to God's faithfulness. Then, in verses 11 and 12, the psalmist receives a new scare, a disaster comes. It is a new trouble, a threat against him. In verses 13 through 17, he prays for deliverance from this new trouble. So the psalm begins with the testimony of deliverance and with a tone of joy, and it ends with a plea for a new deliverance.

A Psalm of Victory and Prayer

Deliverance and Joy

> [1] I waited patiently for the LORD;
>> And He inclined to me, And heard my cry.
> [2] He also brought me up out of a horrible pit,
>> Out of the miry clay,
>> And set my feet upon a rock,
>> And established my steps.
> [3] He has put a new song in my mouth—
>> Praise to our God;
>> Many will see it and fear, And will trust in the LORD.

Waiting in prayer

Describing his manner of prayer, the psalmist says, "I waited patiently for the Lord". The word "wait" signifies to listen intently. That is, when the psalmist says, "I waited patiently", he means that he approached God with an intense expectation. Waiting on the Lord is not passive, it is not to loiter aimlessly. It is an intense wait, like a batter waiting for a pitch. When the batter stands in the batters box, he is waiting for the pitcher, but the batter is anything but passive while he is waiting. This waiting is very intense and expectant. The batters eye is intently focused on the pitcher, and when the ball comes out of the pitcher's hand, the batter becomes focused on the ball. Everything is excluded from the batter's mind. The cheers of the crowd (as well as their jeers) fade away into nothingness. In that brief second that it takes for the ball to reach the batter, nothing distracts the batter; nothing takes his eye off the ball. In the same way, waiting on the Lord is to be focused intently upon him, as we expect him to respond to our prayers. When we wait upon the Lord, we enter our prayer closet and close ourselves off from every distraction. We devote our minds, our hearts, and our energies to the pursuit of God. In return for our intent and singleminded prayer, God promises, "They that wait upon the Lord shall renew their strength; they shall mount up with wings like eagles; they shall run and not be weary; they shall walk and not faint" (Isaiah 40:31).

David, therefore, says, "I waited patiently, intently upon the Lord, and he inclined unto me, and he heard my cry". The word "inclined" means to lean over. The psalmist is describing for us a picture of God leaning over to listen to his prayers, leaning down to get closer, placing his ear near to the one praying. God is very careful to listen, to hear what we have to say. God, as it were, bends over and listens.

The Lord inclined his ear, and he heard the cries of the psalmist. But in the Psalms, it is not enough to say that the Lord *hears* our prayers. God not only *hears* but he also *answers*. The urgent prayers in the Psalms are offered in expectation that God will do more than sympathize—God will act; God will intervene; God will deliver; God will save. I once had a Bible teacher who told us that prayer does not change *things*; prayer changes *us*. While it is true that the practice of prayer is an important part of Christian formation, it is also true that biblical prayer expects an answer. This is not an either or question. Effective prayer changes *things* and it changes *us*. Prayer changes things because God intervenes (see James 5:16-18). An important part of prayer is our petition, in which we ask God to come to our aid. Jesus said, "ask and it shall be given to you" (Matthew 7:7). He did not say, "ask, and will become a better person". He said also, "what things soever you desire you pray, believe that you receive them and you shall have them" (Mark 11:24) and "If you can believe, all things are possible to him that believes" (Mark 9:23).

When we pray, we must believe that God will answer our prayer. If we are in trouble, it's not enough to admit that we are in trouble and to express that to God. It is not enough to ask for the grace to bear the pain and the suffering. Our first intent should be to pray that God will heal the pain, cure the hurt, and deliver us from evil. We are told in James 5 that if any are sick among us, they should call for the elders of the church, who will pray over them, and "the prayer of faith will save the sick", and the Lord will raise them up (James 5:15). When we pray, we should expect God to do something. God will act when we pray.

Of course, we should not pray only when we are in trouble. Prayer should be a habit, a way of life. That is why we are instructed to "pray without ceasing" (1 Thess. 5:17). If we ignore God for days and weeks, then we get in trouble and call out to God, he is by no means obligated to run to our rescue. God is a helper to those who walk with him and to those who are in covenant relationship with him. God hears the prayers of those who delight in his word and who worship him in spirit and in truth. We are God's children, and he looks upon us just as we look upon our own children. If my children have a need and they ask me for help, I gladly supply their need. But if the neighbor's children ask me for help, I weigh more carefully my response. I do not automatically contribute to supplying the needs of all the neighborhood children. I expect their parents to take care of their needs. If I am at the gas station and a young man approaches me and asks me to buy him some gas, perhaps I will and perhaps I will not. But if the young man is my son, I certainly will. We must trust fully in God's love for us and in his desire to supply all of our needs. We should believe God in every situation. This was brought strongly to my attention recently during our church prayer meeting. We prayed for my daughter who had a cyst on her wrist, and it was very painful. A surgeon removed it, but it grew back again. We prayed for her on Sunday night, and the next day the cyst was gone. We are praising God that he answered our prayer and healed our daughter. God is doing the impossible. Let us believe that when we cry to God, he will not just *hear* our cries but also that he will *act* on our behalf.

Lifted out of trouble

The Lord answered the prayer of the psalmist and brought him up out of the horrible pit, out of the miry clay. The psalmist proclaims, "he lifted me up". The pit of which the psalmist speaks was a probably water cistern in which the water was almost gone and deep sticky mud remained at the bottom. The psalmist is standing in the mud and is unable to escape on his own. The pit, of course, is a figure of speech that represents the psalmist's terrible trouble—being in a place where he could not escape. He was stuck in the mud, and there was no way out, but God reached down and lifted him up out of the pit. After he lifted him up out of the pit, he set his feet upon a rock. When God lifted him out of the pit, he did not lift him out in order to set him down somewhere else that was just as dangerous. He lifted him out of danger and set him in a place of safety and security. To be set on a rock is to be set in a steady place, a safe place, a secure place. The rock is firm, and it is dependable. Jesus used the figure of the rock when he talked about building a house. The man who built his house upon a rock was able to withstand the storm the rain and the flood. But the house that was built upon the sand was destroyed by the storms (Matthew 7:24-27).

Given a new song

The psalmist declares that God brought him up out of trouble and set his feet upon a rock, and this deliverance put a new song in his mouth—a song of praise unto God. God gave him a new song. The psalms teach us that deliverance is not complete until we sing about it, until we rejoice in it, until we praise God for it, and until we testify about it to others. God wants our praise. He wants our worship. God's purpose therefore in delivering us is twofold: first he delivers us in order that we might be relieved of the trouble that we are experiencing. Second, he delivers us so that he will be glorified when we tell other people about his mighty deeds. If all we do with God delivers us is to say a simple "thank you Lord", but we do not tell others about it, then half of the blessing is missed. If we do not testify, then the purpose for our deliverance is incomplete. We must testify to what the Lord has done.

Sharing our faith with non-Christians can be scary, especially if those non-Christians are total strangers. However, when we think of witnessing as simply testifying to what the Lord has done for us, then it is not quite so scary. We can be an effective witness for the Lord even if we have not memorized a lot of Scripture verses and even if we are unable to answer every argument that confronts us. We can tell people that we were in a horrible pit, in the miry clay, and God reached down and lifted us out. We can explain how we were blind, but now we can see. We were lost, and now we are found. We can testify to what the Lord has done for us. Personal testimony is a great way of witnessing to people. If we have experienced God's healing, then we should testify that we were sick but God healed us. We can offer to pray with people about their needs and problems. If we can bring people to Jesus, then he will do the rest.

Furthermore, we should sing about God's goodness—not just the old songs but also new songs. When God has delivered us, we have something new to sing about. Sure, we can sing about all the old things that God has done. It is good to recount all of God's blessings as far back as we can remember. In fact, we should write down God's blessings in a journal or notebook, so that in the future we and our children can be reminded of all the things God has done. Sometimes I go back and look at my journal and reflect on what God did for me 20 years ago or 10 years ago or last year. It is very encouraging to know that God has walked with us and helped us throughout our lives.

When we sing, "Many will see it and fear and will trust in the Lord" (v. 3). Our songs and our praises are a witness. When we praise God, when we tell what God has done, other people will be influenced by our experience. They will come to trust in the Lord for themselves on account of our testimony. One of our favorite scriptures in the Pentecostal church says, "Jesus Christ, the same, yesterday, today, and forever" (Hebrews" 13:8). If Jesus healed the sick in Galilee, he will also heal us today. If God answered David's prayers, he will answer our prayers. If he delivered me, he will deliver you. We should hold fast to Jesus and his unchangeable nature.

Psalm 40, therefore, begins as a praise psalm about deliverance. David was in deep trouble, though we do not know the exact nature of his trouble. He does not offer the specifics of his situation; instead, he speaks of his trouble as a deep pit. The pit is probably symbolic, and it may have taken place when he was out in the wilderness, when Saul was chasing after him, or in another similar situation. Because of his song, he says, "many will trust in the Lord". God has done three things for David: (1) he delivered him from the pit; (2) he established him on the rock; (3) he brought joy to his heart and put a song in his mouth.

God's wonderful works

⁴ Blessed is that man who makes the Lord his trust,
  And does not respect the proud,
   nor such as turn aside to lies.
⁵ Many, O Lord my God, are Your wonderful works
  Which You have done;
  And Your thoughts toward us
  Cannot be recounted to You in order;
  If I would declare and speak of them,
  They are more than can be numbered.

In verse 4, David speaks to his audience. He gives a word of encouragement to the hearers of the psalm. Based upon his own experience, David declares that it is wise to trust in the Lord. "Blessed is that man" who trusts in the Lord rather than trusting in people that are proud, people who are deceitful.

In verse 5, David speaks to the Lord. He acknowledges that God is trustworthy and his care for us is beyond words. He says to God, "many are your wonderful works". God's works are many, and they are not only many, they are wonderful. When God does things, they are wonderful because they cause us to be amazed, to stand in wonder and awe of what God can do. As always, we are reminded that God's greatest miracles are his transformations of peoples hearts and lives. It is more difficult for God to change a person's heart than it is for him to heal their physical heart. Of course, all things are possible with God, and from a theological perspective one miracle is not harder than another with him. But from my perspective, a physical healing or the answering of a prayer is a wonderful thing, but it is even more wonderful when God changes people's lives and hearts, especially when he does it instantaneously. He often changes people over a period of time. God reaches out to someone who is against the church and against the gospel, and he begins to work on them. Over a period of time they begin to see God's hand at work and they are finally changed. Other people, however, experience instantaneous transformation. As I reflect upon my own conversion experience, I remember that my life was instantly changed from night to day. One day I cared nothing about God or the things of God—I did not talk about God, I did not think about God; God was the furthest thing from my mind—but the next day, after I gave my heart to Jesus, I woke up with nothing but God on my mind. All I wanted was to praise Jesus, to worship Jesus. I was in love with Jesus. My heart was changed, my affections had been radically transformed. It was an instant change. Whether it takes place instantaneously or gradually, the transformation that God works in a person's life is a wondrous miracle.

Gratitude and Offering

[6] Sacrifice and offering You did not desire;
     My ears You have opened.

> Burnt offering and sin offering You did not require.
> [7] Then I said, "Behold, I come;
>   In the scroll of the book it is written of me.
> [8] I delight to do Your will, O my God,
>   And Your law is within my heart."

The first part of Psalm 40 tells of the psalmist's deliverance and his joy over that deliverance. The next section (vv. 4-5) talks about God's wonderful works. Then, in verses 6-8 David speaks of gratitude and offering. In an earlier chapter, we talked about the vow and the thanksgiving sacrifice. Whenever a person would come to the temple to offer thanksgiving, they would also bring a sacrifice. They would give testimony of God's work, and then offer the sacrifice as a part of their praise. But here David insists that even more important than the offering is obedience. He puts it this way, "I delight to do your will". He longs to do what is right in the sight of God. He adds, "And your law is in my heart". The psalmist has a desire to be faithful to God and to God's word.

Testifying of God's faithfulness

> [9] I have proclaimed the good news of righteousness
>   In the great assembly;
>   Indeed, I do not restrain my lips,
>   O LORD, You Yourself know.
> [10] I have not hidden Your righteousness within my heart;
>   I have declared Your faithfulness and Your salvation;
>   I have not concealed Your lovingkindness
>   and Your truth
>   From the great assembly.

The word of God that is in the psalmist's heart now utters forth from his mouth. He says, "I have proclaimed the good news of righteousness in the great assembly". His proclamation and declaration consists in praise to God for his character and works. When David comes to offer the sacrifice of praise, he realizes that praise is more important than the sacrifice. The praise that comes forth from the heart of the worshiper is more important than the animal that is given to God. This praise comes in the form of a testimony and is proclamation of God's greatness.

The Hebrew word *basar*, translated "proclaimed the good news" is equivalent to the New Testament word *euangelizo*, "to preach the gospel". The word signifies an announcement of victory. The gospel is good news of Christ's victory. It is a proclamation of the good news that Jesus Christ has won the victory over evil. David says that he will proclaim this good news in the "great assembly", that is, in the congregation that has gathered for worship. This was not something he did privately at home. This was not something he did silently in his heart. This was a shout of victory that is proclaimed publicly. He says, "I did not restrain my lips, and I have not hidden your righteousness in my heart, I have told it". If it is in our hearts, then we must speak it forth, tell it, shout it, proclaim it.

The Spirit of God, the flow of God's power in our lives, is not a reservoir to be stored up. It is a river that flows continually. If we try to stop it, hoard it, it will stagnate and it will be useless and worthless. We ask God to fill us, but the filling is a flowing. Our filling is not like the filling of a container; it is like the filling of a pipe. A container is filled in order to keep something, to store it, so it can be used whenever needed. But the Spirit cannot be stored up and set aside, to be used whenever we decide. The Spirit is like the water flowing through a pipe; it flows continually, and it only flows as long as it is connected to the source. For the Spirit to flow through us, we must remain connected to the source, Jesus Christ and the heavenly Father. As long as we remain connected, in the language of the Gospel of John, "abide in him", then out of our innermost being will flow rivers of living water. The Holy Spirit will flow through us. If God has filled us, then we must let him flow through us. We must surrender completely to him and let the Spirit flow in our lives, flow from God through us in ministry to those around us. The flowing of the Spirit through God's people is meant to be a blessing to those who need God and who need God's help. So the psalmist says, "I have not hid it, but I have declared it, I have not concealed it". The writer of Hebrews cites this psalm in talking about Jesus and his elimination of the sacrifices (Heb. 10:1-10). The words of David are placed in the mouth of Jesus, "Lo, I come to do your will, O God" (Heb. 10:9). The writer goes on to explain that Jesus came in fulfillment of Psalm 40 and its implied promise

that sacrifices would be done away with completely. But we see the
hints of that in the book of Psalms already. In addition to Psalm
40, there are other Psalms that suggest the limited value of animal
sacrifices (see, for example Psalm 51).

A new disaster strikes

[11] Do not withhold Your tender mercies from me,
     O LORD;
     Let Your lovingkindness and Your truth
     continually preserve me.
[12] For innumerable evils have surrounded me;
     My iniquities have overtaken me,
     so that I am not able to look up;
     They are more than the hairs of my head;
     Therefore my heart fails me.

Following immediately upon David's praised, we suddenly learn that
the psalmist is in deep trouble again. A new disaster has struck. This
brings us back to verse nine for a moment, where he says, "I have
proclaimed the good news". David asserts his faithfulness in giving
thanks and praising the Lord. By obeying God, by proclaiming
God's works, by testifying, and by giving thanks, David is in a good
position to approach God again. Now that trouble has returned, he
can remind God, "Lord, you know that I have been faithful to testify. I have been faithful to tell what you have done. Now trouble
has struck again and I need your help again." If the psalmist had
not been faithful to offer praise for his previous deliverance, then
he would now have no ground to stand upon in asking for another
deliverance. If he had not testified, if he had not told what God
had done, if he had not given thanks, he would not be able to come
to God with the same level of confidence. If God blesses us and
we do not tell praise him or testify about it, then the genuineness of
our relationship to God may be in question. When we come back to
God at a later time with another serious request, he would be justified in saying to us, "I healed you, I bless you, I provided for you
and you did not give me thanks. You did not praise me." We all appreciate a bit of gratitude when we do something for someone,
even for our own children. When our children are small, we teach

them to say "Thank you". Similarly, we must remember to say "Thank you" to God. God is not human, and therefore does not react like we do, but still he desires our praise. God appreciates our thankful praises. Whenever God blesses us, let us remember to be thankful.

In light of this new threat, the psalmist prays, "Do not withhold your tender mercies from me, O Lord" (v. 11). Why does he need mercy? He explains in the next verse: "My iniquities have overtaken me, so that I am not able to look up; they are more than the hairs of my head" (v. 12). "Iniquity" is another word for sin, so the psalmist is confessing that he has fallen into disobedience. There is a moral failure in his life, and it bears on his mind. He has brought this trouble upon himself. Yes, we sometimes bring trouble upon ourselves because of our unfaithfulness and disobedience or simply because of our lack of wisdom. The Bible tells us that Satan "goes about as a roaring lion seeking whom he may devour" (1 Peter 1:8), and he knows our weaknesses. The enemy knows how to take advantage of our vulnerabilities. In the matter of temptation, we can be our own worst enemy. James tells us that we may be drawn aside by our own lust, and lust brings forth sin. Then sin when it is conceived brings forth death (James 1:14). Sometimes we stumble because we are not paying attention and not walking in the Spirit. If we "walk in the Spirit," Paul says, "we will not fulfill the lust of the flesh" (Gal. 5:16). Sin can overtake us if we are not watchful. But I have good news for you. God knows our weaknesses: "he knows how we are made; he remembers that we are dust" (Psalm 103:14). God knows our frailties; he knows that we need his help. And even when we bring trouble upon ourselves, God cares for us enough to help us if we will call upon him. God is a God of great mercy and grace. If God only helped people who were without fault, then it would be hopeless for all of us. If we have brought trouble upon ourselves, we should repent and seek for God's mercy. God will help us out of our trouble even if we have brought it upon ourselves.

A prayer for God's help

¹³ Be pleased, O LORD, to deliver me;
     O LORD, make haste to help me!

^{14} Let them be ashamed and brought to mutual confusion
    Who seek to destroy my life;
    Let them be driven backward
    and brought to dishonor
    Who wish me evil.
^{15} Let them be confounded because of their shame,
    Who say to me, "Aha, aha!"
^{16} Let all those who seek You rejoice and be glad in You;
    Let such as love Your salvation say continually,
    "The LORD be magnified!"
^{17} But I am poor and needy;
    Yet the LORD thinks upon me.
    You are my help and my deliverer;
    Do not delay, O my God.

The last part of the psalm is David's prayer for help. He admits that he needs to be rescued; he needs to be delivered. He prays, "Help me Lord; please deliver me; make haste to deliver me". He needs God's help, and he wants his suffering to end as soon as possible. And then he gives three wishes for his enemies who are causing his problems. He says, (1). "Let them be ashamed and brought to mutual confusion, those who are trying to kill me". (2). "Let them be driven back and brought dishonor, they who wish me evil". (3). "Let them be confounded, those who say, 'Aha, aha'". He prays that those who are actively seeking to kill him will be put to shame and be brought to confusion. He prays also that those who wish him evil will be driven back and brought to dishonor. Furthermore, he prays that those who are making light of his trouble, those who are laughing over his calamity, will be confounded.

After praying that God will confound his enemies, he turns his attention to a different category of people—those who love the Lord. He prays, "Let all those who seek you rejoice and be glad in you" (v. 16). He hopes that all of God's people will rejoice and be glad, and that everyone who loves salvation will magnify the Lord. His prayer is in the form of a contrast: let the troublemakers be confounded, but let the Lord's people rejoice.

In the last verse he says, "But I am poor and needy, yet the Lord thinks upon me". The poor and needy are often ignored or even shunned in the world, but they are not ignored by God. Yes, the

Lord is thinking about us right now. The songwriter said, "His eye is on the sparrow, and I know he watches me". The Lord is thinking about us. At this moment, we are in his thoughts. We may feel like we are all alone in our trouble. We may feel like we are the only one going through this kind of trouble. Yet none of our troubles are unique; other people suffer the same trials and tests. Though we feel isolated and abandoned, let us remember that God is thinking of us. Many years ago there was a popular song that said, "When he was on the cross, I was on his mind". It is true, and as he hung on the cross, as we were on his mind, his thoughts turned to us in forgiveness, and Jesus prayed, "Father, forgive them for they know not what they do" (Luke 23:34).

The psalmists final words are a confession of faith followed by a concluding plea for God's immediate intervention. He declares, "Lord you are my help and my deliverer", and he pleads, "Do not delay, O my God". Out of his deep distress, he prays for God to answer him speedily. As we walk through the valley, the nights grow darker, and the pain grows deeper. In times of suffering, any delay on God's part seems like an eternity. But we confess with the Apostle Paul that God will not allow us to be tested above that which we are able to bear (1 Corinthians 10:13), and in every trial his "grace is sufficient" (2 Corinthians 12:9).

Conclusion

This Psalm that begins with rejoicing and praise finds the psalmist at the end praying again for help, and some days that is the way our lives work. We get up in the morning and give thanks for another beautiful day, then we get kicked in the shins. But God is faithful. Because the psalmist had praised God for earlier blessings, he now has the confidence to come back to God once again with his need. He is able to trust God, and he has solid ground on which to stand in his plea to the Lord. Let us not fail to praise God when he comes to our rescue so that when we need him again we will have the confidence to call upon his name.

❧ Chapter 7 ❧

The Value of Deep Repentance

Psalm 51

To the Chief Musician. A Psalm of David when Nathan the prophet went to him, after he had gone in to Bathsheba.

[1] Have mercy upon me, O God,
　　　According to Your lovingkindness;
　　　According to the multitude of Your tender mercies,
　　　Blot out my transgressions.
[2] Wash me thoroughly from my iniquity,
　　　And cleanse me from my sin.
[3] For I acknowledge my transgressions,
　　　And my sin is always before me.
[4] Against You, You only, have I sinned,
　　　And done this evil in Your sight—
　　　That You may be found just when You speak,
　　　And blameless when You judge.
[5] Behold, I was brought forth in iniquity,
　　　And in sin my mother conceived me.
[6] Behold, You desire truth in the inward parts,
　　　And in the hidden part You will make me to know wisdom.
[7] Purge me with hyssop, and I shall be clean;
　　　Wash me, and I shall be whiter than snow.
[8] Make me hear joy and gladness,
　　　That the bones You have broken may rejoice.
[9] Hide Your face from my sins,
　　　And blot out all my iniquities.
[10] Create in me a clean heart, O God,

And renew a steadfast spirit within me.
[11] Do not cast me away from Your presence,
And do not take Your Holy Spirit from me.
[12] Restore to me the joy of Your salvation,
And uphold me by Your generous Spirit.
[13] Then I will teach transgressors Your ways,
And sinners shall be converted to You.
[14] Deliver me from the guilt of bloodshed, O God,
The God of my salvation,
And my tongue shall sing aloud of Your righteousness.
[15] O Lord, open my lips,
And my mouth shall show forth Your praise.
[16] For You do not desire sacrifice, or else I would give it;
You do not delight in burnt offering.
[17] The sacrifices of God are a broken spirit,
A broken and a contrite heart—
These, O God, You will not despise.
[18] Do good in Your good pleasure to Zion;
Build the walls of Jerusalem.
[19] Then You shall be pleased with the sacrifices of righteousness,
With burnt offering and whole burnt offering;
Then they shall offer bulls on Your altar.

One goal of this study, is to determine how the Psalms can make us better worshipers. People have different ideas about the nature of worship. Some people believe that worship consists entirely of singing and praising God, but the Psalms teach us that prayer is also an important part of worship. Jesus recognized the necessity of prayer, and he declared, "my house shall be called a house of prayer" (Matthew 21:13, quoting Isaiah 56:7). The Apostle Paul, instructing young pastor Timothy about proper worship, writes, "Therefore I exhort first of all that supplications, prayers, intercessions, and giving of thanks be made for all" people (1 Timothy 2:1).

Not only must prayer be a vital component of every worship service, prayer must be a part of our preparation for worship. Through his prayer of confession in Psalm 51, David prepares his heart to reenter the presence of God. In the Old Testament, the priests were required to wear clean white robes and to wash their hands before entering the temple. Sacrifices were offered that cleansed the temple and represented a cleansing of people's sins. The purity of heart that is required of worshipers is emphasized in Psalm 24, which says, "Who may go up unto the hill of the Lord? Who may stand in his holy place? He who has clean hands and a pure heart, who has not lifted up his soul unto vanity nor sworn deceitfully. He shall receive blessing from the Lord" (v 3-4). Before we proceed to worship God, we should examine our hearts and pray for cleansing and purification.

Jesus spoke a parable to those who trusted in themselves that they were righteous and despised others. He said,

> Two men went up to the temple to pray, one a Pharisee and the other a tax collector. The Pharisee stood and prayed thus with himself, 'God, I thank You that I am not like other men— extortioners, unjust, adulterers, or even as this tax collector. I fast twice a week; I give tithes of all that I possess.' And the tax collector, standing afar off, would not so much as raise his eyes to heaven, but beat his breast, saying, 'God, be merciful to me a sinner!' I tell you, this man went down to his house justified rather than the other; for everyone who exalts himself will be humbled, and he who humbles himself will be exalted" (Luke 18:10-14).

Confession of sin is not easy for some Pentecostal believers. We have taught rightly that Christians should be sanctified and live in victory over the power of sin. However, the emphasis on victorious living has made us hesitant to admit our failings. We do not want to admit that we have sinned. We have been taught that whoever is born of God does not continue to commit sin (1 John 3:9). There- fore, sin cannot habitual behavior for the Christian. However, we also read that anyone who claims to have no sin is deceived (1 John 1:8). The good news for all of us is that if we sin, "we have an ad- vocate with the Father, Jesus Christ the righteous" (1 John 2:1), and if we "confess our sins, he is faithful and just to forgive us our sins, and to cleanse us from all unrighteousness" (1 John 1:9). Our spiri- tual grandfather John Wesley taught that sanctified Christians do not willingly and actively pursue sin. Nevertheless, he insisted that because of our weaknesses everyone commits unwitting sin every day. So he taught his followers to pray for daily cleansing and daily forgiveness of sins.

I would suggest that the first thing that we do when we enter the presence of God is to ask him to search our hearts for anything that is unpleasing to him. As we come into worship, we should ask the Lord to cleanse us—to cleanse our hearts so that we may worship him without any barrier between us. In Psalm 139, David prays, "Search me, O God, and know my heart: try me, and know my thoughts: And see if there be any wicked way in me, and lead me in the way everlasting" (vv. 23-24). As we come into worship, let us pray that nothing in our lives will be withheld from God, so that we may worship freely and openly with liberty in the Spirit. Let us pray that there be no hindrance in our lives, no selfishness, no deceitfulness, no guile, that our hearts will be open completely to God. Prayers of repentance are essential for a Christian. To pray and ask God's forgiveness is necessary.

A Psalm of Repentance

The heading of the psalm

To the Chief Musician. A Psalm of David when Nathan the prophet went to him, after he had gone in to Bathsheba.

This psalm is a personal prayer of repentance, what we might call a penitential Psalm or a penitential lament. The heading situates this prayer in the life of David as a repentant response to the prophet Nathan's rebuke (2 Samuel 12:1-14). The Psalm has been used by Jews and Christians for hundreds of years as a model for repentance. Whenever we need to pray a prayer of deep repentance and ask for God's forgiveness, we can use this Psalm is a way of approaching God in prayer. It is an example of how we, as God's people, can come to the Lord for forgiveness, cleansing, and restoration when we have stumbled and fallen.

A plea for mercy

[1] Have mercy upon me, O God,

> According to Your lovingkindness;
> According to the multitude of Your tender mercies,
> Blot out my transgressions.
> ² Wash me thoroughly from my iniquity,
> And cleanse me from my sin.

David does not mince words. He gets right to the point, "Have mercy upon me, O God". In Hebrew, very first word of Psalm 51 is "grace"—used in the form of a verb. The English language does not have a verb that signifies the giving of grace. But the Hebrew word here is a verb, and David's prayer might be translated literally, "Grace me, O God", "Favor me, O God", "Be gracious to me, O God", or "Show me grace, O God".

This is a powerful way to begin the Psalm. David does not waste words making futile excuses. We are tempted to offer one excuse or another: "I was trying", or "I did my best", or "I will do better next time". But when seeking God's forgiveness, all excuses are prideful and pointless. Our human human efforts will never be sufficient; rather we must learn to rest in the grace of God. We must throw ourselves at the foot of the cross, and cry out to God, "Have mercy upon me a sinner". We need God's grace. There is no other hope except grace.

David does not compare his righteousness with that of others. The basis of his plea is not "Be gracious to me, Lord, because I am a better man than my neighbor". Instead, he prays pointedly, "O God, give me grace". In our pleas for pardon we must not argue that we are improving or making progress. No, we must plead for grace. There is no other way to forgiveness. There is no other hope for healing. Forgiveness and freedom come by grace alone.

David does not make excuses for his sin, and neither does he base is prayer upon his rank, position, status, or title. The basis of his plea is not, "God, give me grace because I am the king of Israel"? He does not argue, "God, give me grace because I found myself in a bad situation?" Instead, his request for God's grace is based upon God's "lovingkindness" and "mercy". Therefore, the basis of grace and forgiveness is the nature of God. God's nature is love. It is God's nature to be gracious and merciful and compassionate. The Hebrew word for "lovingkindness" *hesed*, which signifies covenant love or covenant faithfulness.

By using the word *hesed*, "covenant faithfulness", David demonstrates that he considers himself to be already in a covenant relationship to God. That is, he is one of God's people, so his is not the prayer of an unbeliever. It is very important that we understand that David's repentance is not of someone who has been outside the church, outside the body of Christ, outside the congregation, outside of the congregation of believers. David is a believer. He is one of God's people. He is a part of the congregation, but he has done wrong. And he says, "God, have mercy upon me according to your covenant faithfulness".

The focus here is not upon David's faithfulness but upon God's faithfulness. We do not come to God in worship based upon our faithfulness, we come to God in worship trusting in God's faithfulness. And again, we must realize that our salvation, the ground of our forgiveness, the ground of our pardon, is our promise to do better. Of course, true repentance assumes a transformation of heart and a change of direction. But grace is not given on the basis of our self-improvement. Grace is given out of God's love to us.

Using different words, David repeats his request: "According to the multitude of Your tender mercies, blot out my transgressions. The words "tender mercies" might also be translated "affectionate compassion". David's petition is based upon God's compassion, affection, and love as the ground of forgiveness.

Furthermore, he says, "blot out my transgressions"— "According to your affection for me, according to your compassion, wipe out the record of my evil choices". It is as if his sins were written down, and he is asking God to wipe them out, to erase them from a tablet. "Erase my sins", he pleads. David repeats his request for forgiveness using two other parallel terms: "wash" and "cleanse". He prays, "Wash me thoroughly from my iniquity. Cleanse me from my sin".

In addition to his use of three words to signify forgiveness, he also uses three different words for sin, just to make it clear that he knows what he has done. First, he uses the word "transgression" (Heb. *pesha*), which means a breaking of God's law, disobedience to God's commandments. Second, he uses the word "iniquity" (Heb. *avon*), which means a twisting or distorting of what is right. Some scholars think that it refers to waywardness or corruption. Third, he uses the word "sin" (Heb. *chatah*), which is a deviation from God's commandments. These multiple words display the multifaceted nature of sin. Is sin a rebellion against God? Yes. Is it a distortion of what is right? Yes. Is sin a deviation from God's commandments? Yes. Sin is all of these things and more, that is why the Old Testament includes so many different terms that specify the different aspects of sin—transgression, iniquity, sin. They all refer to what happens when a person departs from God's will and God's commandments. David uses all three words. He confesses that he is guilty of every aspect of sin. He recognizes the magnitude of his guilt, therefore, he presents four requests to God: (1) "Be gracious to me". (2) "Blot out my transgressions". (3) "Wash me from my iniquity". (4) "Cleanse me from my sin". David knows the depth of his failure; he sees the urgency of his plight; and he desperately wants to be thoroughly and completely cleansed and purified.

The pain and depth of sin

³ For I acknowledge my transgressions,
    And my sin is always before me.
⁴ Against You, You only, have I sinned,
    And done this evil in Your sight—
    That You may be found just when You speak,
    And blameless when You judge.
⁵ Behold, I was brought forth in iniquity,
    And in sin my mother conceived me.
⁶ Behold, You desire truth in the inward parts,
    And in the hidden part You will make me to know wisdom.

David says literally, "I know my transgressions". That is, he is being constantly reminded of his disobedience and his failure. It is ever on his mind. And he admits to God, "Against you, you only have I sinned, and done this evil in your sight". In his admission he adds a fourth word for sin: "evil" (Heb. *ra*). David's actions were "evil" in the sight of God. The Hebrew word "evil" suggests that David's disobedience produced harmful consequences—to himself, to his relationship with God, and to other people besides himself. He hurt other people.

David insists that, ultimately, his sin is against God alone. It is clear from Scripture that when we sin, we hurt other people and that we can sin against people. Therefore, David does not intend to say that his actions did not hurt other people. He is saying essentially that he cannot bring back from the dead Uriah the Hittite, whom he murdered; and his adultery cannot be undone. All he can do is ask God, whom he has offended, to restore the broken relationship between God and David. Once have sinned, we cannot undo it, but we can ask God for a restoration of fellowship.

David adds, "that you may be just when you speak and blameless when you judge" (v. 4). Paul cites this verse as a way of explaining that our sin proves that God is righteous in his judgment of us (Rom. 3:4). None of us is righteous because "all have sinned and come short of the glory of God" (Rom. 3:23). When God judges us, therefore, he is just, he is righteous in his judgment. He is blameless. But thankfully, Paul can add the assurance that "where sin abounded, grace did much more unbound" (Rom. 5:20).

The psalmist continues to deepen his confession: "I was brought forth in iniquity, and in sin my mother conceived me". He recognizes that his sin problem consists of more than one action, more than one weakness. In fact, his entire life is permeated by the influence of sin. Even before he was born, sinfulness was a part of him, residing in his nature. This is what theologians call original sin or the sin nature. As soon children can begin to make choices, they will make the wrong choice. As soon as they have the capability to obey or disobey, they will choose to disobey. As soon as they have the ability to move, they will move in the wrong direction. As soon as they have the ability to speak, they will tell a lie. Sin is pervasive in the fallen human nature and it is serious. David admits that his problem is more than the commission of one sin, but that his whole life has been influenced by sin, and he needs constantly to come to God for cleansing, for purging, for help. He needs God's grace; he needs God's mercy.

A plea for thorough cleansing

7 Purge me with hyssop, and I shall be clean;
    Wash me, and I shall be whiter than snow.
8 Make me hear joy and gladness,
    That the bones You have broken may rejoice.
9 Hide Your face from my sins,

And blot out all my iniquities.

The earnestness of David's plea for cleansing is manifested in his repetition. It is not enough that he asks once for forgiveness; he must ask again and again. This time he says, "Purge me with hyssop and I shall be clean". To "purge" is to remove all traces of contamination and defilement. He asks that he be purged with hyssop. Hyssop is a plant, an herb, a small bush, which was used in purification ceremonies. The bushy plant was dipped in the blood of the sacrifice, which was then sprinkled upon the person or object that need to be purified. It was first used on the day of Passover, when the Israelites dipped the hyssop in the blood of the sacrificial lamb and applied the blood onto the doorpost and to the top of the door (Exodus 12:22). Later on, when Moses confirmed God's covenant with the people at Mount Sinai, he took the sacrificial blood, dipped the hyssop in the blood, and sprinkled it upon the people as confirmation (Exodus 24:8). The hyssop here is a symbol of cleansing because it is used to apply the blood of cleansing. David's request, "purge me with hyssop", is a figure of speech, because it is not the hyssop that cleanses his sins, rather it is the blood that is on the hyssop that cleanses. So David's prayer here is a reference to the cleansing power of the blood of the sacrifice.

He prays further, "Wash me and I will be whiter than snow". Snow is a well known symbol of purity. Nothing is cleaner than freshly fallen snow. The prophet Isaiah utilized the same symbol when he wrote, "Come now, and let us reason together, saith the Lord: though your sins be as scarlet, they shall be as white as snow; though they be red like crimson, they shall be as wool" (Isaiah 1:18).

The psalmist then asks, "Make me hear joy and gladness" (v. 9). David's guilt has robbed him of joy. The weight of his sin prevents him from enjoying the usual pleasures of life and the spiritual blessings that come in times of worship.

David again asks for forgiveness, this time saying to God, "Hide your face from my sins, and blot out my iniquity".

David shows in verses six through nine that he desires more than just forgiveness. He asked to be forgiven, then he asks to be clean. In other words, beyond being freed from the *penalty* of sin, he wants to be cleansed from the *presence* of sin. We should not be satisfied to say that we are forgiven and that we will escape hell, the punishment for our sins. God intends for us a life of fullness and joy in his presence. We should desire to be clean before God, to be pure in heart. Jesus died on the cross to forgive us of our sins but also to "redeem us from all iniquity and purify" us as his special people (Titus 2:14). The Lord promised this cleansing when he spoke through the prophet Ezekiel: "Then will I sprinkle clean water upon you, and ye shall be clean: from all your filthiness, and from all your idols, will I cleanse you" (Ezekiel 36:25). Let us pray for complete cleansing from sin.

A plea for inner renewal

[10] Create in me a clean heart, O God,
　　And renew a steadfast spirit within me.
[11] Do not cast me away from Your presence,
　　And do not take Your Holy Spirit from me.
[12] Restore to me the joy of Your salvation,
　　And uphold me by Your generous Spirit.

The word "create" is used in the Bible only of God. Only God can create. We may try to reform the heart, turn the heart, appeal to the heart, and teach the heart. But only God can create a clean heart. David's request for a clean heart reminds me of Jeremiah's prophecy of the new covenant:

> Behold, the days come, saith the LORD, that I will make a new covenant with the house of Israel, and with the house of Judah ... I will put my law in their inward parts, and write it in their hearts; and will be their God, and they shall be my people ... for I will forgive their iniquity, and I will remember their sin no more (Jeremiah 31:31-34).

Ezekiel uttered a similar prophecy regarding God's plan to create a new heart in his people:

> A new heart also will I give you, and a new spirit will I put within you: and I will take away the stony heart out of your flesh, and I will give you an heart of flesh. And I will put my Spirit within you ... and ye shall be my people, and I will be your God (Ezekiel 36:26-28).

God promises more than forgiveness and more than cleansing; he promises the creation of a new heart. God promises to give his people a new heart that loves God, a new heart that desires to serve God. It is a heart that will be filled with God's Spirit. It will be the fulfillment of David's prayer, "create in me a steadfast spirit".

Then in verse 11, David pleads, "Do not cast me away from your presence". Here he asking for a restored relationship. David, of course, knew what happened to Saul. When King Saul continued to behave in defiance to God's clear directions, God rejected him as king, and the Spirit of the Lord left him. When Spirit of the Lord departed from him and an evil spirit came upon him, Saul virtually lost his mind. He became mentally unstable. David's prayer suggests that he may have been thinking about Saul's failure, and he may have been hoping that God would not reject him as well. Therefore, he prays, "Do not take your Holy Spirit from me". There is nothing more tragic than a person who was once filled with God's Spirit but now is empty because the Spirit has departed. It is a terrible thing to lose touch with God.

A promise to testify

[13] Then I will teach transgressors Your ways,
   And sinners shall be converted to You.
[14] Deliver me from the guilt of bloodshed, O God,
   The God of my salvation,
   And my tongue shall sing aloud of Your righteousness.
[15] O Lord, open my lips,
   And my mouth shall show forth Your praise.

Having confessed his sins thoroughly and having repented deeply, David begins to look forward. He says, "Then ..." When he is forgiven, *then* he will teach others. When he is cleansed, *then* sinners will be converted. Once the joy has been restored to him, *then* he will praise God. After God has created in him a new heart, *then* he will use his voice to bless other people. After he has been delivered from the "guilt of bloodshed", *then* he will "sing aloud" of God's righteousness. *Then*, he says, "my mouth will show forth your praise."

Brokenness and sacrifice

¹⁶ For You do not desire sacrifice, or else I would give it;
    You do not delight in burnt offering.
¹⁷ The sacrifices of God are a broken spirit,
    A broken and a contrite heart—
    These, O God, You will not despise.
¹⁸ Do good in Your good pleasure to Zion;
    Build the walls of Jerusalem.
¹⁹ Then You shall be pleased with the sacrifices of righteousness,
    With burnt offering and whole burnt offering;
    Then they shall offer bulls on Your altar.

David knows that sacrifices are not sufficient to forgive sins. David understands that the Old Testament sacrifice was an outward symbol of inward faith and repentance. The Old Testament does not teach salvation through the sacrifices, as some people have mistakenly taught. God requires that the sacrifice be accompanied by faith and true repentance. The apostle Paul argued in Romans that the Old Testament believers were justified by faith just as we are (Genesis 15:6). The sacrifices were meant to represent a person's repentance, and look forward to the sacrifice of Jesus on the cross. In the book of Hebrews it says that the Old Testament sacrifices did not put away sin and did not cleanse the conscience. They only represented forgiveness. The person was still required to repent. David, therefore, argues that God does not really demand sacrifice and burnt offerings. He knows that what God really wants in us is a broken spirit, a broken and a contrite heart.

Only the Spirit of God can break our hearts so that we can turn to God. It is more than a matter of our will; it is more than a matter of our making a decision in our mind. Of course, the will and the mind are involved in repentance, but the Holy Spirit must draw us to God. Jesus said, "No one can come to me, except the Father who has sent me draw him" (John 6:44). It is the Father, through Holy Spirit, who draws us to the Savior. Whenever we feel the Holy Spirit tugging at us to draw closer to God, we must not resist. When the Spirit draws us, that is the time to respond.

Finally, the psalm closes with a prayer that God will strengthen the walls of Jerusalem, the holy city. After the city is secured, God will "be pleased with the sacrifices of righteousness, with burnt offering and whole burnt offering; then they shall offer bulls" on the altar of the temple (v. 19). Most Bible scholars tell us that these last two verses were added to the psalm after the Babylonian captivity when Jerusalem had been destroyed and there was no temple. In that period of time, like today, they could not offer sacrifices. Today, the Jews do not offer sacrifices because they do not have a temple. So these last two verses are essentially a prayer to God that he will bring about the rebuilding of the temple on Mount Zion and that he will bring about the restoration of the sacrifices.

These last two verses do not stand in contradiction to David's previous statement that God does not desire sacrifice. We know that David did offer sacrifices. Again, we note that this is poetry and one of the literary devices of poetry is to make a very strong statement in order to prove your point, all the while knowing that it is a hyperbole (that is an intentional exaggeration for emphasis). Therefore, when David says to God, "you do not desire sacrifice", we understand it to mean that God does not desire a sacrifice that is detached and separate from genuine repentance. The sacrifices were meant to facilitate repentance and they were meant to lead the worshiper to the state of brokenness. David knows that what God wants more than anything is our repentant heart. And that the sacrifices are just symbols.

The Old Testament sacrifices functioned in a manner similar to the way water baptism functions today. We do not believe in baptismal regeneration. That is, we do not believe that water baptism produces the new birth. We do not believe that water baptism alone produces the forgiveness of sins that we need. But we believe that along with our repentance and conversion we should be baptized, because baptism represents our cleansing from sin and our death to the old way of life. Water baptism represents conversion but it does not produce conversion. It represents a change of heart. It represents death and resurrection—the resurrection of new life as a Christian. As Paul puts it, anyone who is in Christ Jesus "is a new creature: old things are passed away; behold, all things are become new" (2 Corinthians 5:17). Therefore, in a way similar to David's prayer, we might say to God, "Lord, you do not desire water baptism; you desire genuine repentance". Still, God commands that we be baptized. And in the Old Testament he still wanted the sacrifices, though his ultimate aim was in the creation of a new heart. Of course, animal sacrifices are not a part of the new covenant. But we still offer sacrifices. What is our sacrifice? Our sacrifices are two-fold: first, we present our "bodies a living sacrifice" (Romans 12:1); second, we offer "the sacrifice of praise to God continually" (Hebrews 13:15).

Psalm 51 is a powerful example of confession and repentance. If we have anything in our lives that we need to confess to God, David's words can be a model for us to follow in reaching out to God for his grace and mercy. We must allow the Holy Spirit work in our lives, and we must pray for every obstruction between us and God to be removed. Then, when our hearts have been cleansed by God's grace, we can enter into his presence and worship him in Spirit and in truth.

Conclusion

We have now studied three psalms of lament: Psalm 13, Psalm 22, and Psalm 51. We noted several characteristics of the laments that are present in Psalm 51. First, that the laments normally speak directly to God, just as David does here. He prays, "Be gracious to me, O God".

Second, we also observed that the lament expresses the pain of abandonment, a theme that is registered in David's words, "Do not cast me away from your presence, and do not take your Holy Spirit from me. Restore to me the joy of your salvation" (vv. 11-12). To be cast away from God's presence and to be void of God's Spirit would surely signify utter abandonment. David's prayer that he might again "hear joy and gladness" suggests that he is living in misery because God has cut him off from his presence.

Third, we pointed out that the lament will name the complaint, the problem, the burden. In Psalm 61 the complaint, the problem, is David's sin and its resultant guilt and distress.

Fourth, the lament pleads for God's intervention through the use of specific petitions. This element of the lament is found throughout Psalm 51. David asks that his sins be forgiven, that his heart be cleansed, and that his relationship with God be restored.

Fifth, the lament flows out of a trusting relationship, and usually there is a statement of confidence or trust. Oddly enough, there is no explicit statement of confidence or trust in this Psalm. However, David implies trust what he prays on the basis of God's "loving kindness". Therefore, he is trusting in God's loving kindness, which signifies God's covenant faithfulness. Further trust is implied in verse fourteen when David addresses God as "God of my salvation". If God is the God of salvation then it implies confidence and trust.

Sixth, there is usually in the lament a statement of assurance that the psalmist has been heard and that God will answer. A clear statement of assurance is lacking in this Psalm. However, David promises that when he is forgiven, "then" he will teach others. He promises that he will help others to find grace just as he found grace.

Seventh, the lament normally concludes with a commitment to praise God, which is found here in verses 13 through 15.

Although several of the elements of the lament are not conspicuous in Psalm 51, we should not be surprised. As we pointed out earlier, the writers of the Psalms, while utilizing some standard formulations, were free to express their prayers and their praises in individual ways. The parts of the lament that are not as distinct and filled out as in other psalms may be lacking because this Psalm almost from the first word to the last, is permeated by a plea for forgiveness and restoration. It is almost totally a prayer. In its nineteen verses, David utters fifteen requests. Most of the laments devote no more than one or two verses to the specific petitions. But the prayer for forgiveness in Psalm 51 is repeated over and over. David's request for forgiveness is passionate, deep, and urgent; therefore, repetition is necessary. His guilt weighs heavily upon his mind and heart, and this prayer of repentance is in part a means of working through the process of self-examination, and self-criticism until he reaches a place of complete honesty and openness with God.

The psalmist is serious about confessing his sin because sin is a serious matter. Alienation from God is not a matter to be taken lightly. The prayer of Psalm 51 prayer is not generated out of duty or out of daily habit; rather, it pours forth from the heart that is crushed by the effects of sinful choices. It is not a "now I lay me down to sleep" type of prayer. The psalmist understands the severity of his sin and suffers its distressful consequences. He knows that he has done wrong, and he wants God to know that he is truly, honestly, and deeply repentant.

In the complaint section of the laments, there is usually a complaint against God himself, such as "How long will you forget me, O Lord?" (Psalm 13:1) or "My God, My God, why have your forsaken me?" (Psalm 22:1). In many laments there is a complaint of sickness, or a complaint against an enemy, but not here. In Psalm 51 the only enemy is the psalmist himself. His own sin is his greatest problem. David is his own worst enemy.

Ultimately, we are to blame for the choices we make. We are responsible for the path that we take. We are the only ones who can choose to do right or to do wrong. Therefore, our problem may not be with God, with sickness, with trials, or with enemies. Our most severe battle is the battle inside us, within our hearts. And that truth makes Psalm 51 very powerful.

Chapter 8

Approaching God with Hard Questions

Psalm 73
A Psalm of Asaph.
[1] Truly God is good to Israel,
    To such as are pure in heart.
[2] But as for me, my feet had almost stumbled;
    My steps had nearly slipped.
[3] For I was envious of the boastful,
    When I saw the prosperity of the wicked.
[4] For there are no pangs in their death,
    But their strength is firm.
[5] They are not in trouble as other men,
    Nor are they plagued like other men.
[6] Therefore pride serves as their necklace;
    Violence covers them like a garment.
[7] Their eyes bulge with abundance;
    They have more than heart could wish.
[8] They scoff and speak wickedly concerning oppression;
    They speak loftily.
[9] They set their mouth against the heavens,
    And their tongue walks through the earth.
[10] Therefore his people return here,
    And waters of a full cup are drained by them.

[11] And they say, "How does God know?
     And is there knowledge in the Most High?"
[12] Behold, these are the ungodly, Who are always at ease;
     They increase in riches.
[13] Surely I have cleansed my heart in vain,
     And washed my hands in innocence.
[14] For all day long I have been plagued,
     And chastened every morning.
[15] If I had said, "I will speak thus,"
     Behold, I would have been untrue to the generation of |
     Your children.
[16] When I thought how to understand this,
     It was too painful for me—
[17] Until I went into the sanctuary of God,
     Then I understood their end.
[18] Surely You set them in slippery places;
     You cast them down to destruction.
[19] Oh, how they are brought to desolation, as in a moment!
     They are utterly consumed with terrors.
[20] As a dream when one awakes, So, Lord, when You awake,
     You shall despise their image.
[21] Thus my heart was grieved,
     And I was vexed in my mind.
[22] I was so foolish and ignorant;
     I was like a beast before You.
[23] Nevertheless I am continually with You;
     You hold me by my right hand.
[24] You will guide me with Your counsel,
     And afterward receive me to glory.
[25] Whom have I in heaven but You?
     And there is none upon earth that I desire besides You.
[26] My flesh and my heart fail;
     But God is the strength of my heart and
     my portion forever.
[27] For indeed, those who are far from You shall perish;
     You have destroyed all those who desert You for harlotry.

²⁸ But it is good for me to draw near to God;
>   I have put my trust in the Lord GOD,
>   That I may declare all Your works.

Have you ever heard anyone say, "You need to get your head on straight?" Well that is what Psalm 73 is all about—getting our heads on straight. To put it in more theological terms, this psalm presents worship as a revisioning of reality. That is, worship helps us to see reality as God sees it, not as humans see it.

Spiritual realities are not easily recognized, as Elisha's servant learned when he and Elisha were surrounded by Syrian soldiers. The servant was afraid, and Elisha says, "Do not fear, for those who are with us are more than those who are with them." Then Elisha prayed, and the Lord opened the eyes of the servant, and he saw that "the mountain was full of horses and chariots of fire all around Elisha" (2 Kings 6:16-17). This story of Elisha and his servant illustrates the possibility of different perceptions of reality. The reality seen by Elisha was different from the reality seen by the servant.

We learn from Hebrews 11 that spiritual realities are often invisible to the natural eye. We read that "faith is the substance of things hoped for and the evidence of things not seen" (Heb. 11:1). If things are "not seen", can they be real? The answer, of course, is yes, they are real. Abraham searched for a country and a city that he had never seen (Heb. 11:8-10). When Moses left Egypt, "he endured as seeing him who is invisible" (Heb. 11:27).

Psalm 73 demonstrates that when we enter into the presence of God, he changes our perception of reality. Being in the presence of God changes our understanding of what is right and what is wrong, what is good and what is bad. Being in the presence of God changes our perception of who we are in relation to God. In the presence of God the truth is made known, secrets of the heart are unveiled, wickedness is condemned, lies are exposed, and hypocrisy is judged. But also, in the presence of God the wounded are healed, the poor are lifted up, the weary are strengthened, the grieving are comforted, and the fearful are encouraged. In the presence of God, our perception of reality stripped of all pretense, and the truth is made evident. In his presence, God becomes everything, encompassing both the beginning and the end of all things.

Hard Questions

The heading of Psalm 73

A Psalm of Asaph.

The Psalter is divided into five books, and Psalm 73 is the first psalm in the the Book Three. Book Two closes with the words, "The prayers of David the son of Jesse are ended" (Psalm 72:20), thus marking the end of a certain collection of David's Psalms, particularly his prayers. That does not mean, however, that there are no more Psalms of David in the book of Psalms, it just means that Psalm 72 is the end of one collection of the Psalms of David. Psalm 73 is a Psalm of Asaph, who is named in the headings of twelve psalms. Eleven of those twelve psalms are in Book Two of the Psalter; the other is in Book Two (Psalm 50). Asaph is described in 1 Chronicles as a musician who worked in the temple as one of David's worship leaders (6:31-39). He apparently led a group of singers and musicians who were known by the name, "the sons of Asaph" (1 Chronicles 25:1-2).

The accepted truth

[1] Truly God is good to Israel,
>   To such as are pure in heart.

Psalm 73 is narrates four steps in a process of growth in the life of the psalmist.
>   1. Foundational belief—God is good to his people.
>   2. Contradictory observation—The wicked prosper.
>   3. Reality revisioned—God will set things straight.
>   4. Renewed faith—Asaph will trust in God.

Step one begins with the accepted truth that God is good to Israel and to those who are of a pure heart. Asaph's foundational belief is our belief as well. In step two, the psalmist's established belief is challenged when he sees the prosperity of the wicked. He reasons that if God is good to the pure in heart, if God punishes the wicked, then why is it that the wicked appear to prosper? Step three is Asaph's entrance into the sanctuary of God, and there the truth of God's goodness to him is renewed. There in the sanctuary of God he sees the end of the wicked. Finally, in step four, Asaph appropriates the truth to himself. The last verse says, "It is good for me to draw near to God. I have put my trust in the Lord God". So he has come full circle, God is good and it is good for him to be close to God. It is good for him to be close to God and to trust in the Lord. These are the main points in the Psalm, and as we go through this Psalm we can see how the message develops.

The psalm begins with a powerful statement, "Truly, God is good to Israel, to such as are pure in heart". We find other verses very similar to this throughout the Bible:

"Taste and see that the Lord is good; blessed is the man who trusts in him" (Psalm 34:8)

"For the Lord is good; his mercy is everlasting" (Psalm 100:5)

"Praise the Lord, for the Lord is good" (Psalm 135:3)

"Praise the Lord of hosts for the Lord is good" (Jeremiah 31:11)

"The Lord is good to those who wait for him" (Lamentations 3:25)

"The Lord is good, a stronghold in the day of trouble, and he knows those who trust in him" (Nahum 1:7)

Psalm 1 tells us that the righteous are blessed and the wicked are doomed. The righteous person is "like a tree planted by the rivers of water", and everything he does will prosper (Psalm 1:3). The wicked, however, are "like the husk that the wind drives away" (Psalm 1:4), and they have no place in the congregation of the righteous. "The Lord knows the way of the righteous, but the way of the wicked will perish" (Psalm 1:6). The very first Psalm, therefore, tells us that God will bring wicked people to destruction but that God is watching over his people to take care of them, and to bless them. Psalm 73 begins with the same assurance—God is good to Israel, to those who are of a pure heart.

The truth is challenged

² But as for me, my feet had almost stumbled;
    My steps had nearly slipped.
³ For I was envious of the boastful,
    When I saw the prosperity of the wicked.

Asaph believes in God's goodness, but when he sees wicked people who appear to be doing well, he is troubled. Therefore, he admits that he "almost stumbled" and he was "envious" of the wicked because he saw their prosperity. The Hebrew word for "prosperity" here is "*shalom*", which means wellness and wholeness. When he observes the wicked, they show all the signs of health, wealth, and happiness. There is no evidence that they are suffering under the judgment of God at all. It looks as if God is blessing them. Of course that is his perception. Envy, jealousy, and covetousness are dangerous attitudes that can color our view of reality. We imperil our own spiritual health when we compare ourselves (and our possessions) with other people. It is then that our feet may slip, and we may tumble into the kind of envy that the psalmist talks about here. It is good, however, that the psalmist his envy of the wicked and the negative results of that envy. The first step to finding a solution is to admit our need.

Description of the wicked and their prosperity

⁴ For there are no pangs in their death,
    But their strength is firm.
⁵ They are not in trouble as other men,
    Nor are they plagued like other men.
⁶ Therefore pride serves as their necklace;
    Violence covers them like a garment.
⁷ Their eyes bulge with abundance;
    They have more than heart could wish.
⁸ They scoff and speak wickedly concerning oppression;
    They speak loftily.
⁹ They set their mouth against the heavens,
    And their tongue walks through the earth.

Asaph does not stop with his admission of envy toward the wicked. He expands on his description of their abundance, their extravagance, and their pride. In verses four through nine, the psalmist enumerates at least four specific areas where he sees the wicked prospering. First, the wicked do not suffer at their time of death like many of the good people that he knows. Apparently, he is arguing that they can afford the best doctors, the finest comforts, and the most expensive food and drink. Perhaps they have servants to attend to their needs. Because of all these advantages he does not think they are suffering. He sees their strengths, and they do not seem to be in trouble as other men are. They are not plagued like other men. This is his perception of these wicked people.

Second, they are not in "trouble" neither are they "plagued" like other people. Because of their wealth, they have no financial problems. They need not worry if the weather will turn bad or if their crops will come up short. They have more than enough. Their fine houses and new clothes will protect them from the cold and from disease. If one of their animals dies, they will hardly miss it.

Third, Asaph speaks of their pride. These wicked people are proud, boastful, and violent. They wear their pride unashamedly like a necklace and their violence covers them like a garment. The theme of pride is picked up again in verses eight and nine. They "scoff" and "speak loftily" about their wicked exploits. These evil people take advantage of those who are weaker. They boast in their wickedness. Furthermore, they are so arrogant that they speak against God himself. They "set their mouth against the heavens." They believe they are all-powerful. He does not identify these powerful people, so we have to assume that they are either people in the community who are disobeying God's laws and are oppressing their neighbors, or they are enemies who have invaded Israel, such as the Assyrians and Babylonians.

Fourth, he observes their wealth. He says, "Their eyes bulge with abundance". They eat so much that their eyes are popping out. Food was not as abundant in the ancient world as it is in today's Western societies. In biblical times, most of the people barely subsisted from one crop to another, and hunger was a very present reality. If the crops did not make, the people faced many difficult months, and some of them might even starve to death. There was no food bank, food stamps, community centers, or welfare. Asaph says of the wicked that they have more than their heart could wish. He knows that some righteous people do not have enough, yet these wicked people have too much.

The suffering of God's people

[10] Therefore his people return here,
And waters of a full cup are drained by them.
[11] And they say, "How does God know?
And is there knowledge in the Most High?"
[12] Behold, these are the ungodly, Who are always at ease;
They increase in riches.

Asaph sees the comfortable lives of the wicked, and he sees also the suffering of God's "people" (v. 10). His statement that "the waters of a full cup are drained by them" appears strange and cryptic to us. He seems to be saying that God's people are so poor that they could not spare one drop out of a cup of water. They will drink every drop of a cup of water because they may not get any more. In ancient times, all drinking water would come either from a stream or a well. Therefore, the bottom of the cup would likely contain a bit of dirt or dregs, which would not be consumed. But he is saying here that they would train their cups dry because they are so poor. They do not want to leave any to waste. They do not want to waste a drop because it is so precious to them.

The confusion of the psalmist

[13] Surely I have cleansed my heart in vain,
And washed my hands in innocence.
[14] For all day long I have been plagued,
And chastened every morning.

The psalmist observes the ungodly, always at ease and increasing riches. He reasons that it is pointless to serve God. "Surely," he says, "I have cleansed my heart in vain and washed my hands in innocence". In other words, he considers his efforts to serve God to be in vain. He has been faithful to God, but he sees no benefit in his faithfulness. He is doing everything that he can to live according to God's commandments, but he is suffering. His rich neighbors are not obeyed God, and they seem to be blessed. So what is the point of living for God? The observation of the psalmist seems to be in contradiction to the promise of Psalm 1, where we hear that the righteous person is like a tree, planted by rivers of water, which brings forth fruit, his leaf does not wither, and whatsoever he does prospers.

Despite all his efforts to maintain a clean heart and clean hands (which symbolize actions), he continues to be "chastened every morning" and "plagued" all day long. Even though he is living faithfully, he feels like he is suffering all the time.

The struggle of the psalmist in Psalm 73 reminds me of Satan's question to God in Job 1. When Satan speaks to God about Job he says, "Does Job serve God for nothing?" He then says, "If you will take away all the things that you have given Job he will curse you." So God allows Satan to take away Job's possessions, his property, and his family. Everything is snatched from Job, but Job does not curse God. Instead he says, "The Lord gave and the Lord takes away, blessed be the name of the Lord" (Job 1:21). If the Lord gives to us, we should praise him. If he takes it away, we should praise him still. Jesus encourages us to focus upon spiritual things rather than the material. He says, "Your life consists of more than the clothes you wear or the food you eat" (Luke 12:23). Therefore, let us praise him.

Meeting God

The truth renewed in God's presence

¹⁵ If I had said, "I will speak thus,"
    Behold, I would have been untrue to the generation of |
    Your children.
¹⁶ When I thought how to understand this,
    It was too painful for me–
¹⁷ Until I went into the sanctuary of God,
    Then I understood their end.

Asaph believes that something is wrong with the reality that he observes in the world. Something is wrong when the wicked are prospering and the righteous are suffering. He recognizes possible harmful consequences of voicing his doubts publically. If he were to speak about his skepticism then, then he "would have been untrue to the generation" of God's children. That is, he does not want to discourage other people. Perhaps Asaph writes from the perspective of his role as a leader among the worship leaders. He does not want to discourage the people who are under his leadership. This is a good lesson for those of us who are in leadership and for parents and teachers. Unfortunately, some people seem to enjoy bringing discouragement and gloom wherever they go. There seems to be a dark cloud hovering over their heads. And every time they open their mouth they suck the life and the joy out of everything. We should not speak everything that comes to our minds, particularly when it may produce detrimental effects on other people. We would be wise to keep some of our thoughts to ourselves. Scripture advises us, "Do not be rash with your mouth, And let not your heart utter anything hastily before God. For God is in heaven, and you on earth; therefore let your words be few" (Ecclesiastes 5:2). The psalmist is rightly concerned about other people and what effect his words will have upon them.

Asaph is trying to make sense of what he had observed in the world. He is asking himself why the wicked are prospering and why the righteous are suffering. He is troubled by his thoughts. He says, "When I thought how to understand this, it was too painful for me" (v. 16). His mind could not handle the apparent contradiction. Asaph was not the first nor the last to struggle with these questions. The matter of God's justice and righteousness has been studied by all of the world's greatest philosophers, and none of them yet have figured it all out. Books have been written by the hundreds trying to explain why righteous people suffer. But there are some things that we cannot understand.

In his troubled state, Asaph entered the "sanctuary", the house of God. The psalmist comes into the sanctuary of God seeking for light and for answers to his difficult questions. There, in the presence of God, his understanding is expanded, and he sees a different picture of the wicked. He finds peace of mind when sees "their end". Asaph does not explain exactly how this transformation happens. He says simply, "I went into the sanctuary". The psalmist is talking about the power of worship, the transforming power of being in the presence of God. He is demonstrating and testifying to the fact that encountering God in worship is more than a ritual, more than meaningless habit. The psalmist is telling us that worship causes us to see the world differently. In worship, our entire perspective changes. He went into the sanctuary, then he understood. We do not know if he heard some kind of teaching, if he heard a prophecy, or if he heard someone reading the Scripture. We do not know if he heard someone praying, or he heard a praise or a testimony. Perhaps David was there, and David took out his harp and began to sing, "The Lord is my shepherd; I shall not want, he maketh me to lie down in green pastures. He restores my soul." Perhaps he heard someone singing Psalm 27, "The Lord is my light and my salvation, whom shall I fear; the Lord is the strength of my life, of whom shall I be afraid. When my enemies and my foes came upon me to eat up my flesh, they stumbled and fell. Though a host should encamp against me, in this I will be confident." Whatever happened, it was in the presence of God, as he worshiped before the Lord and beheld the beauty of the Lord and the power of the Lord, that God turned him around. He came in depressed, and he went out lifted up. He came in down, but he left with his head held high. He could have contacted the Bible scholars to give him the explanation, but they would have revealed nothing new. But there in the sanctuary of God, he received a new view of reality. It was not through any change of the circumstances, but through a change of his spiritual understanding, a change of his spiritual location, that he sees the world differently. Being in the presence of God changes our outlook on the world.

Psalm 73 reminds me of Job's experience. Throughout the entire book of Job, he and his "friends" attempt to determine the reason for Job's suffering. They cannot understand why so many tragedies have befallen him. Job questions God and seeks for explanations. But then at the end of the book of Job, God appears and begins to tell of all his greatness. He says to Job, "Were you there when I put the stars in place? Were you there when the morning stars sang together?" God expounds upon his majesty, his power, and his glory, and Job says, "I have heard about you with my ears but now my eyes have seen you, and I repent in dust and ashes." Job went away from that encounter with God a changed man, a happy man, a satisfied man, a content man. But we notice that God never answered his questions. When Job entered the presence of God, the questions no longer seemed so important.

The questions themselves begin to fade into nothingness when we enter into the presence of the Lord. In the book of Revelation, the Apostle John is exiled on the island of Patmos. In a vision, he sees the troubles coming upon the world. But then, God says to John, "Come up here". Up he goes to the throne room of God, and from God's throne room the entire world looks different. There in the presence of God, John's perspective changes. Similarly, we read in the book of Isaiah that in the year that King Uzziah died, the prophet Isaiah went to the house of God. No doubt he was concerned about the death of the king and the future of the kingdom. But then Isaiah says, "I saw the Lord, high and lifted up. And his train filled the temple and his glory was everywhere". His encounter with the presence of the Lord changed Isaiah's life.

We might recall the experience of the disciples after Jesus rose from the dead. Jesus visited with them for 40 days, and he told them to wait in Jerusalem until they were clothed with power from heaven. Therefore, they went to the temple to pray and worship, but they were afraid, and they had no direction. Still, they gathered together and waited as the Lord had told them. Then the day of Pentecost came, and they were all filled with the Holy Spirit. No longer were they afraid and no longer were they fearful. Immediately, they began to go throughout the land preaching the gospel. Why? Because they had an encounter with the presence of God that gave clarity to their mind, direction to their life, and purpose for their actions. The threats had not disappeared; in fact, Peter and John were soon arrested and forbidden to preach. As soon as they were released, they returned to the church, and everyone gathered together to pray. There in prayer the Holy Spirit came down again, and we read that they were all filled with the Holy Spirit, and they spoke the word of God with boldness. They were still under the threats, and many of them gave their lives, but they did not care because they were in the presence of the Lord. That is what a difference it makes when we come into God's house and encounter his presence.

Can you testify to a similar experience? I can. Many times we have faced questions, difficult circumstances, and needed answers. Then, we entered the house of God, and we worshiped God, and we sought God. At some point during that service of worship, God reached out and touched us. He may not have answered our prayers immediately, and he may not have given us answers to all of our questions, but because God came down and touched us, we received a new vision of reality. When we entered the worship, we were at the point of giving up, but we departed with new strength. We came in sick, but we went out healed. In God's presence, this renewal can happen in a moment, in an instant. It can happen in various ways: it can be a song, it can be a Scripture, it can be the sermon, it can be a testimony, it can be a kind word of a member of the congregation, or it can be a prayer. God can speak to us through a song. It can happen through the preaching. It can happen to us as we are reading our Bibles. It can happen to us as someone beside us prays for us. Through whatever means it happens, ultimately it is the presence of God in the sanctuary of worship that transforms us. It is God's Holy Spirit that does a work in our hearts. Genuine worship is powerful. Worship is not entertainment. Worship is not a distraction, like watching television. Worship is an encounter with God, and we are changed by that encounter. Reflecting upon his own experience, David says to the Lord in Psalm 30, "You have turned for me my mourning into dancing; You have put off my sackcloth and clothed me with gladness."

The end of the wicked

[18] Surely You set them in slippery places;
    You cast them down to destruction.
[19] Oh, how they are brought to desolation, as in a moment!
    They are utterly consumed with terrors.
[20] As a dream when one awakes, So, Lord, when You awake,
    You shall despise their image.

In the sanctuary, Asaph began to view the wicked in a different light. He says, "Then I understood their end". The wicked seem to prosper, but where do they end up? What is the end of their story? What is the end of their life? The Psalmist learned that it is important not how we begin but how we end. The justice God may come slowy, but it will come. He sets the wicked "in slippery places." He said earlier that his feet almost slipped, but now he says it is the

wicked who are slipping and sliding. Furthermore, God casts down
the wicked "to destruction", and in a moment they are utterly consumed.

The psalmist reflects upon the experience

^{21} Thus my heart was grieved,
    And I was vexed in my mind.
^{22} I was so foolish and ignorant;
    I was like a beast before You.
^{23} Nevertheless I am continually with You;
    You hold me by my right hand.
^{24} You will guide me with Your counsel,
    And afterward receive me to glory.
^{25} Whom have I in heaven but You?
    And there is none upon earth that I desire besides You.
^{26} My flesh and my heart fail;
    But God is the strength of my heart and
    my portion forever.

Looking back on his experience, the psalmist grieves over his for-
mer attitude. He realizes that he had been "foolish and ignorant".
He had envied the prosperity of the wicked; he had allowed discouragement to set in; and he had become depressed and bitter. He
admits that his envy had caused him to start doing foolish things
and speaking out in ignorance. He says to God, "I was so foolish
and ignorant, I was like a beast". But God did not reject Asaph.
God is "continually" with him, holding his hand and guiding him
into a brighter future. "Afterward", the Lord will receive him "to
Glory". The word "afterward" is the same word as "end". When he
went into the sanctuary, he learned the "end" of the wicked. The
end of the wicked is destruction, but the end the righteous is glory.
    Continuing to address God, the psalmist says, "Whom have I in
heaven but You? And there is none upon earth that I desire besides
You." God is guiding him, holding his right hand; therefore, what
else does he need? At first, he had apparently desired to be prosperous like the wicked people whom he envied. But now, he desires
only God. He desires to know God, to walk with God, and to be in
the sanctuary of God. Even when his physical body breaks down,

when his "flesh and heart fail", God will be his strength and his "portion".

The truth appropriated in life

²⁷ For indeed, those who are far from You shall perish;
  You have destroyed all those who desert You for harlotry.
²⁸ But it is good for me to draw near to God;
  I have put my trust in the Lord GOD,
  That I may declare all Your works.

Even though Asaph had seen the wicked prospering, he now concludes that all those who are "far from" God "shall perish". God
will destroy all those who are unfaithful and who desert God for
"harlotry". Harlotry is a figure of speech that represents the forsak-
ing of God for the worship of other gods, the worship of idols.
Those who have forsaken God and have been unfaithful to God
will be destroyed.

 Asaph does not want to be one of those who is "far" from god.
He wants just the opposite—to be close to God. He says, "It is
good for me to draw near to God". As he draws near to God, he
will also put his "trust in the Lord" and "declare" all of God's
works. The psalmist had earlier refused to speak, because he did not
want to discourage other believers with his negative observations.
Now, however, his heart overflows with a different kind of word, a
word of praise. Now, his questions no longer are important. Now,
he is able to talk of God's "works". He will tell what God has done
so that they can experience the same help that he experienced, so
they can enjoy the same transformation that he have experienced.
He will tell everyone what the Lord has done for him, that they also
may be blessed. As we have said before, the blessings of God are
not just for us, but God blesses us so that we can bless others. We
bless others with our testimonies and by sharing what God has
done.

Conclusion

Right in the middle of the book of Psalms we have an example of
the journey of faith. Psalm 73 begins with Asaph's trust in the

goodness of God and his belief that evil is punished and good is rewarded. His initial theology is that of Psalm 1, in which the righteous are blessed and the wicked are doomed. But Asaph's theology is challenged by the inconsistencies that he observes around him. Just as we saw in Psalm 13, 22, and 40, the psalmist notices that the righteous often suffer unjustly. God's people encounter troubles, while the wicked seem to prosper. In Psalm 73, Asaph moves from confidence in his hopeful theology into a period of doubt and discouragement. He then enters the sanctuary of God, where the Lord restores his faith and hope.

We learn from Psalm 73 that the truth will be challenged and we will face serious questions. How will we handle the questions?—By entering the sanctuary of God. In worship, the clouds are scattered; our hearts are renewed; and hope is reborn.

Chapter 9

Bless the Lord, O My Soul

Psalm 103

A Psalm of David.

¹ Bless the LORD, O my soul;
     And all that is within me, bless His holy name!
² Bless the LORD, O my soul,
     And forget not all His benefits:
³ Who forgives all your iniquities,
     Who heals all your diseases,
⁴ Who redeems your life from destruction,
     Who crowns you with lovingkindness and tender mercies,
⁵ Who satisfies your mouth with good things,
     So that your youth is renewed like the eagle's.
⁶ The LORD executes righteousness
     And justice for all who are oppressed.
⁷ He made known His ways to Moses,
     His acts to the children of Israel.
⁸ The LORD is merciful and gracious,
     Slow to anger, and abounding in mercy.
⁹ He will not always strive with us,
     Nor will He keep His anger forever.
¹⁰ He has not dealt with us according to our sins,
     Nor punished us according to our iniquities.
¹¹ For as the heavens are high above the earth,
     So great is His mercy toward those who fear Him;
¹² As far as the east is from the west,
     So far has He removed our transgressions from us.

¹³ As a father pities his children,
>   So the LORD pities those who fear Him.
¹⁴ For He knows our frame;
>   He remembers that we are dust.
¹⁵ As for man, his days are like grass;
>   As a flower of the field, so he flourishes.
¹⁶ For the wind passes over it, and it is gone,
>   And its place remembers it no more.
¹⁷ But the mercy of the LORD is from everlasting to everlasting
>   On those who fear Him,
>   And His righteousness to children's children,
¹⁸ To such as keep His covenant,
>   And to those who remember His commandments
>   to do them.
¹⁹ The LORD has established His throne in heaven,
>   And His kingdom rules over all.
²⁰ Bless the LORD, you His angels, Who excel in strength,
>   who do His word, Heeding the voice of His word.
²¹ Bless the LORD, all you His hosts,
>   You ministers of His, who do His pleasure.
²² Bless the LORD, all His works,
>   In all places of His dominion.
>   Bless the LORD, O my soul!

What does it mean to "Praise the Lord"? Or, in light of the opening words of Psalm 103, what does it mean to "Bless the Lord?" We will attempt to answer that question as we begin this chapter with a discussion of some of the Hebrew words that are related to the subject of worship.

Words of Worship

Worship

The first word that we will discuss is "worship" (*havah*), which in Hebrew means to pay homage to God, to bow before God, or to honor to God. It is the basic word that means to give God the adoration and praise that he deserves. For example,

And Abraham said to his young men, "Stay here with the donkey; the lad and I will go yonder and worship, and we will come back to you" (Genesis 22:5).

Give unto the LORD the glory due to His name; **worship** the LORD in the beauty of holiness (Psalm 28:2).

All the earth shall **worship** You And sing praises to You (Psalm 66:4).

Oh come, let us **worship** and bow down; Let us kneel before the LORD our Maker (Psalm 95:6).

Give Thanks

A second word related to worship is "to give thanks" (*yadah*). Giving thanks, or "thanksgiving", refers to giving public praise to God for specific actions that he has done. We talked about this word in relation to Psalm 30, which we used as an example of the Psalms of Thanksgiving, where the psalmist talks about specific answers to prayer. Thanksgiving is testifying about God's work that he has done on our behalf. Examples include:

And she conceived again and bore a son, and said, "Now I will **give thanks** to the LORD." Therefore she called his name Judah (Genesis 29:35).

Sing praise to the LORD, You saints of His, And **give thanks** at the remembrance of His holy name (Psalm 30:4).

I will give You **thanks** in the great assembly; I will praise You among many people (Psalm 35:18).

Praise

A third worship word is "praise" (Heb. *hallal*). The word "praise" often signifies the kind of praise that is given to God for his character, his nature, and his attributes. The qualities of God's greatness, his majesty, his care, his grace, and his mercy are all worthy of our praise. Scholars call this type of praise "descriptive praise", as we mentioned earlier. This kind of praise uses words that describe God. For example, we praise God because he is loving, merciful, kind, gracious, good. All of these words are words in praise of his character. The word "praise" in some of the ancient near Eastern languages was used in a secular context for cheering, like the cheering on of athletes. It is a general word that acknowledges someone's greatness. It means to boast about the qualities of God. Whenever we are praising God, we are in effect cheering for him. We are cheering, "Hoorah for God! God is great. God is mighty! God is wonderful!" Examples include:

I will call upon the LORD, who is worthy to be **praised** (2 Samuel 22:4).

And he appointed some of the Levites to minister before the ark of the LORD, to commemorate, to thank, and to **praise** the LORD God of Israel (1 Chronicles 16:4).

I will give You thanks in the great assembly; I will **praise** You among many people (Psalm 35:8).

I will **praise** the name of God with a song (Psalm 69:30).

Praise the LORD! Oh, give thanks to the LORD, for He is good! (Psalm 106:1)

From the rising of the sun to its going down The LORD's name is to be **praised** (Psalm 113:3).

Praise the LORD! Sing to the LORD a new song (Psalm 149:1).

Let everything that has breath **praise** the LORD. Praise the LORD! (Psalm 150:6)

Exalt

A fourth worship word, one which is used less frequently, is the word "exalt" (Heb. *rum*). "Exalt" (sometimes translated "extol") means to "lift up or raise up high". It means to lift up God and to acknowledge that he is great. It means to praise him because he is the highest in power and authority in goodness and greatness. He is the highest of all. Of all things. He is above everything, high and lifted up. This is what we mean when we say that we exalt God. The word "exalt" is used in the following Scriptures:

The LORD is my strength and song, And He has become my salvation; He is my God, and I will praise Him; My father's God, and I will **exalt** Him (Exodus 15:2).

"The LORD lives! Blessed be my Rock! Let God be **exalted**, The Rock of my salvation! (2 Samuel 22:47)

Be **exalted**, O LORD, in Your own strength! We will sing and praise Your power (Psalm 21:13).

I will **extol** You, O LORD, for You have lifted me up, And have not let my foes rejoice over me (Psalm 30:1).

Be **exalted**, O God, above the heavens; Let Your glory be above all the earth (Psalm 57:5).

Exalt the LORD our God, And worship at His footstool -- He is holy (Psalm 99:5).

Magnify

Fifth is the word "magnify" (*gadal*), which means "to make great" or to "proclaim his greatness". While "exalt" has to do with height, "magnify" has to do with greatness. The following Scriptures use the word "magnify":

Oh, **magnify** the LORD with me, And let us exalt His name together (Psalm 34:3).

I will praise the name of God with a song, And will **magnify** Him with thanksgiving (Psalm 69:30).

Let the LORD be **magnified** (Psalm 35:27).

And let those who love Your salvation say continually, "Let God be **magnified**!" (Psalm 70:4)

Your eyes shall see, And you shall say, "The LORD is **magnified** beyond the border of Israel" (Malachi 1:5).

Glorify

Sixth, when we worship, we "glorify" God (Hebrew *kabed*). To "glorify" God is to praise him because he is glorious. All glory and honor belongs to him. The word "glory" (*kabod*) refers to his majestic presence, his weighty presence and his awesomeness. His awesome presence is his glory, so when we say, "Lord, I glorify you", we mean that we are proclaiming him as majestic, glorious, and magnificent. Notice the following Scriptures:

You who fear the LORD, praise Him! All you descendants of Jacob, **glorify** Him (Psalm 22:23).

All nations whom You have made Shall come and worship before You, O Lord, And shall **glorify** Your name (Psalm 86:9).

I will praise You, O Lord my God, with all my heart, And I will **glorify** Your name forevermore (Psalm 86:12).

Therefore **glorify** the LORD in the dawning light (Isaiah 24:15).

For the LORD has redeemed Jacob, And **glorified** Himself in Israel (Isaiah 44:23).

Bless

A seventh worship word, which David uses here in Psalm 103, is "bless" (*barak*). To bless God means to acknowledge or praise God as the source of all our blessings, whether it be specific or general. That is, as God blesses us, we bless him by conceding that all we have comes from him. All that we are, he made us. Every good thing in our lives has its origin in the grace of God. We acknowledge him as the source and the power behind all that is good in our lives. We notice that in Psalm 103, David enumerates a long list of God's blessings. He blesses God for "all his benefits", for forgiving his "iniquities", for healing his "diseases", for saving him from "destruction", for crowning him with "lovingkindness and tender mercies", and for satisfying his "mouth with good things" so that his youth is "renewed like the eagle's".

All of the good things that come to us are blessings from God, and to bless him is to confess and to proclaim and to praise him for all of his goodness toward us. Other examples of blessing God include the following:

When you have eaten and are full, then you shall **bless** the LORD your God for the good land which He has given you (Deuteronomy 8:10).

Then David said to all the assembly, "Now **bless** the LORD your God." So all the assembly **blessed** the LORD God of their fathers, and bowed their heads and prostrated themselves before the LORD and the king (1 Chronicles 29:20).

Stand up and **bless** the LORD your God Forever and ever! **Blessed** be Your glorious name, Which is exalted above all **blessing** and praise! (Nehemiah 9:5)

I will **bless** the LORD at all times; His praise shall continually be in my mouth (Psalm 34:1).

But we will **bless** the LORD From this time forth and forevermore. Praise the LORD! (Psalm 115:18)

Lift up your hands in the sanctuary, And **bless** the LORD (Psalm 134:2).

Sometimes the psalmist will combine these and other praise words together in order to make an impact. Also, it is important to remember that even though these words have specific emphases, they are sometimes used as synonyms in parallel to one another. That is, they sometimes overlap in meaning.

The word "fear" also has to do with worship. To fear him means that we reverence him as the highest authority over our lives. To fear something means that we give it prominence, and we are to give prominence only to God. We should not fear sickness, or even death, because God is greater than death. We should not fear poverty, because God promised to supply our needs. To fear God means that we recognize that God is above every other thing in the universe and nothing can touch us, nothing can hurt us, if God is with us. That is why Jesus said, "Do not fear men who can kill the body, but fear God who can cast both body and soul into hell".

To worship, to give thanks, to praise, to bless, to exalt, and to magnify—each of these acts of worship can be accomplished verbally with our mouth, physically with clapping or dancing, and musically through playing of instruments and singing. But the genuineness of worship can be judged only by the sincerity of the heart. Jesus warned the Pharisees, "Hypocrites! Well did Isaiah prophesy about you, saying: These people draw near to Me with their mouth, and honor Me with their lips, but their heart is far from Me" (Matthew 15:7-8). The Pharisees valued the outward appearance, the performance and the ritual. They would stand on the street corner and pray a long prayer, so that people would know how holy they were. When they fasted, they would not wash their face and they would not comb their hair. They would look disheveled, and they would appear to be grieving. True worship must come forth from the heart.

Bless the Lord, O my soul

The theme of Psalm 103: Bless the Lord

[1] Bless the LORD, O my soul;
> And all that is within me, bless His holy name!

David begins this psalm by setting forth a theme that runs throughout to the end of the psalm. His theme is "Bless the Lord, O my soul". The phrase, "O my soul", is very interesting because it signifies that David is talking to himself. Earlier, we looked at the thanksgiving psalms, in which the psalmist testifies to the congregation. But in this case, he is talking to himself and calling upon himself to bless the Lord.

When David speaks of his "soul", he is not referring to his inner person only. The Hebrews did not have the concept of a divided person. They did not see the human being as a body which has a soul and a spirit. The Hebrew concept is that a person is a living soul, a unity. That is why the apostle Paul uses the phrasing, "your whole body soul and spirit", emphasizing the wholeness of humanity. The word "soul" means the living person. In Genesis chapter 2, God breathed into Adam, and he became a living soul, meaning a living person, a whole person. So when David says, "Bless the Lord, O my soul", he is saying, "Bless the Lord, my whole person". We do not usually talk to ourselves this way, but it is not uncommon in the Bible. He is exhorting himself to bless the Lord. "Self", David says, "bless the Lord. Self, praise the Lord". Then he adds, "and all that is within me, bless his holy name". Everything that is inside of us should shout the praises of God. Our minds, hearts, feelings, thoughts, and will. He is exhorting himself to worship God through and through. This is not shallow worship, outward ceremony, or empty ritual. This is not the kind of worship where we are daydreaming, with our minds wandering. This is worship that is coming from deep inside, with all our hearts, all of our minds, and all of our strength. All that is within us should bless his holy name.

The reason for praise: All God's kindnesses

[2] Bless the LORD, O my soul,
>   And forget not all His benefits:
[3] Who forgives all your iniquities,
>   Who heals all your diseases,
[4] Who redeems your life from destruction,
>   Who crowns you with lovingkindness and tender mercies,
[5] Who satisfies your mouth with good things,
>   So that your youth is renewed like the eagle's.

Next, David gives a number of good reasons for praise—"Forget not all of his benefits". He is reminding himself that he must not forget what God has done. When the Israelites began to cross over the Jordan River into the promise land, Joshua warned them saying,

> So it shall be, when the LORD your God brings you into the land of which He swore to your fathers, to Abraham, Isaac, and Jacob, to give you large and beautiful cities which you did not build, houses full of all good things, which you did not fill, hewn-out wells which you did not dig, vineyards and olive trees which you did not plant -- when you have eaten and are full— then **beware, lest you forget** the LORD who brought you out of the land of Egypt, from the house of bondage (Deuteronomy 6:10-12).

This is exactly what the psalmist is saying to himself, "Self, do not forget what God has done for you". It is easier than we think to forget what God has done. When we began to struggle, and when we begin to have troubles and conflicts and problems and burdens, we begin to focus on those things, and we forget what God has done. We forget to praise him for those blessings. This Psalm teaches us to remember what God has done.

David does not want to forget all of God's "benefits". In Hebrew word "benefits" is really a broader term that refers to all of God's dealings with us. It means "recompense" or "payment"; it is God's response to our situation. God responds carefully and graciously to our circumstances, and let us not forget it. Therefore, the focus of this Psalm is upon blessing God for his attentiveness in dealing with us.

We should "bless the Lord" for all his dealings with us, but how does he deal with us?" He forgives our iniquities; he heals our diseases, he redeems us from destruction (vv. 3-4). He deals with us in righteousness and justice (v. 6). Later in this psalm, David says, "He has not dealt with us according to our sins, nor punished us according to our iniquities" (v. 10). That is, he deals with us mercifully, graciously, and compassionately (v. 8). He deals with us like a father deals with his children (v. 13). Throughout Psalm 103, David is explaining how God deals with his children.

David's list of divine benefits deserves further comment. First, the Lord "forgives all of your iniquities". The word "iniquity" means wrongdoing. God forgives our acts of wrongdoing. The word "forgive" means to pardon. A pardon is different from an acquittal. On the one hand, an acquittal is a judgment that a person is not guilty of the crime with which the person has been charged. On the other hand, a pardon is a release from the legal consequences of an offense or conviction. God knows our sins; he knows that we are guilty as charged; yet he pardons us; he forgives us because of his mercy and grace. He forgives all of our iniquities.

Not only is the Lord the one "who forgives all your iniquities", he is the one who "heals all your diseases". Perhaps David remembers the word of promise that the Lord spoke to Israel in the days of Moses: "For I am the LORD who heals you" (Exodus 15:26). Just as God's forgiveness is available equally to all kinds of sin, his healing is available to cure all kinds of diseases. According to David, the Lord's "benefits" extend to both the spiritual and physical realms. Furthermore, David does not refer to forgiveness and healing in the past tense, as if he had received them only once. He perceives them as continuing gifts from God. David blesses God because God is his "forgiver" and his "healer".

David then adds another reason to bless God, "He redeems your life from destruction". The Hebrew word translated "destruction" is literally "the pit", which means the pit of death. In this context, redemption means to deliver and liberate from the power of death and the grave.

After forgiving, healing, and redeeming, God "crowns you with lovingkindness and tender mercies". This crown is an item of beautification and decoration, intended to show that he honors us. In congratulations for victory, he puts on our heads a crown of loving kindness and tender mercy. He beautifies us by crowning us with spiritual blessings.

Still another reason to bless God is that "he satisfies your mouth with good things." To satisfy means to make full or make overflowing. These "good things" will cause your youth to be "renewed like the eagle's".

God saves the oppressed and forgives the sinner

[6] The LORD executes righteousness
　　And justice for all who are oppressed.

[7] He made known His ways to Moses,
     His acts to the children of Israel.
[8] The LORD is merciful and gracious,
     Slow to anger, and abounding in mercy.
[9] He will not always strive with us,
     Nor will He keep His anger forever.
[10] He has not dealt with us according to our sins,
     Nor punished us according to our iniquities.

Until now, the psalmist has been speaking to himself, encouraging himself to "bless the Lord". But now he points beyond himself to include all of God's people. The bigger work of God is that he "executes righteousness and justice for all who are oppressed." As a specific example, he reminds us of the exodus from Egypt—"He made known his ways unto Moses, his acts unto the children of Israel." In the time of Moses, the Israelites were "oppressed" by the Egyptians, but God delivered them from Egypt. God vindicated them and judged righteously that they were being mistreated.

Israel's salvation from Israel from Egypt symbolizes and prefigures all of God's later acts of deliverances. In the same way that God saved Israel from the bondage of Egypt, he comes down and delivers us from the bondage of sin. As sinners, we were "taken captive" by the Devil (2 Timothy 2:26). But Jesus "delivered us from the power of darkness and conveyed us into the kingdom of" of God (Colossians 1:13). When we were in bondage to sin and darkness, Jesus found us, rescued us from darkness, and carried us into his kingdom. He set us free.

To Moses and to the Israelites, "He made known his ways" as a savior and deliverer. He made known to them all his "benefits", his ways of dealing with his people. How does God deal with his people? He saves his people from bondage; he forgives them, heals them, redeems them and beautifies them.

David's affirmation that the Lord is "merciful and gracious" is a reflection back on one specific occasion when God "made known his ways unto Moses". It was the time when Moses requested to see God's "glory" (Exodus 33:18). The Lord put Moses in the cleft of the rock, and "passed before him and proclaimed, The LORD, the LORD God, merciful and gracious, longsuffering, and abounding in goodness and truth, keeping mercy for thousands, forgiving iniquity and transgression and sin, by no means clearing the guilty" (Exodus 34:6-7). The Lord revealed himself to Moses as a God who is merciful and gracious, a God who is slow to anger, but abounding in mercy.

The psalmist adds further that God "will not always strive with us, nor will he keep his anger for ever". The words "strive" means to bring an accusation against someone, and in this context it has reference to God's covenant with Israel. If Israel breaks the terms of the covenant, then God has the right to be angry and to bring an accusation against them. But David says here that God will not continue accusing his people, nor will he remain angry with them. That is why John said, "If we confess our sins, he is faithful and just to forgive us of our sins, and to cleanse us from all unrighteousness" (1 John 1:9). Yes, our unfaithfulness angers God, but he does not stay angry. He is a compassionate and merciful God.

God's mercy is expressed in verse 10: "He has not dealt with us according to our sins nor punished us according to our iniquities". God deals with us in light of his love, grace, and mercy. He knows that we are sinners, but he does not deal with us on that basis alone. The word used here for "sins" is the general Old Testament word that means missing the mark. God has a standard, and we have missed it. The word "iniquities" means to intentionally do something wrong (see discussion on v. 3). We might say there are intentional sins and there are unintentional sins—sins of omission and sins of commission. Unfortunately, sin is something that comes naturally; we can sin without even trying. We are born as sinners, we do not have to learn to sin. David encourages us to bless the Lord because, although we are sinners, God does not deal with us according to our sins.

God's grace is beyond comparison

[11] For as the heavens are high above the earth,
　　So great is His mercy toward those who fear Him;
[12] As far as the east is from the west,
　　So far has He removed our transgressions from us.
[13] As a father pities his children,
　　So the LORD pities those who fear Him.

David uses three figurative expressions to show that God's grace is beyond comparison. First, "as the heavens are high above the earth, so great is his mercy" toward us. As we stand upon the earth, the heavens are unreachable, far beyond our grasp. Similarly, the mercy of God is greater than we can even imagine. Second, "as far as the east is from the west, so far has he removed our transgressions from us". In David's mind, the east and the west are opposite ends of the earth. East and west never meet. Third, "as a father pities his children, so the Lord pities those who fear him". A good father has infinite compassion on his children, and that is the extent of the Lord's compassion upon us. Because God's grace is beyond comparison, one expression is not sufficient to illustrate it. The psalmist must use three comparisons in order to come close to expressing the grace of God. Yet, even these are not sufficient. God's mercy is higher than the heaven is above the earth. He has removed our sins as far from us as the east is from the west. Like a father cares for his children, that is how much the Lord cares for us.

God knows our finiteness

[14] For He knows our frame;
        He remembers that we are dust.
[15] As for man, his days are like grass;
        As a flower of the field, so he flourishes.
[16] For the wind passes over it, and it is gone,
        And its place remembers it no more.

Having praised God for his incomparable grace, David now turns to the finiteness of humanity. God is heavenly, but he knows that we are earthly. God is eternal, but he knows we are mortal. He knows that we are finite, mortal, and limited. God "knows our frame; he remembers that we are dust." The frame that we are built upon is the dust of the earth. From the dust we are made and unto dust we will return (Genesis 3:19). God made us and he knows exactly what we are. He knows we are dust.

Not only are we earthly, made of dust, but we are also temporary like grass. As the grass and the flowers pass quickly away, dried up by the wind, so we live only a short time. The flowers flourish, but then "the wind passes over it, and it is gone", and we see no sign of it after that. We are like the grass and the flowers. We are limited, temporal, and mortal. We are here one day and gone the next. Our life is like a vapor "that appears for a little time and then vanishes away" (James 4:14).

God's grace is infinite

[17] But the mercy of the LORD is from everlasting to everlasting
On those who fear Him,
And His righteousness to children's children,
[18] To such as keep His covenant,
And to those who remember His commandments
to do them.

After the brief comments on finite human existence, David returns to God's infinite grace. We are finite but God is infinite—his mercy "is from everlasting to everlasting". We may be like the flower that comes and goes, but God's mercy is for ever. From age to age he is the same. "From everlasting to everlasting" he is God (Psalm 90:2). God extends his "righteousness to children's children". The blessings of God go even beyond our own personal life to that of our children. God's mercy reaches to our children and to our grandchildren. We do not have to worry about our children because God's mercy is big enough to take care of our children and their children.

The mercy of God is infinite and the grace of God is beyond comparison, but in return for his mercy and grace, God expects love, loyalty, and worship. He insists that we honor him, respect him, and reverence him. David states that we must "fear" the Lord (vv. 11, 13, 17), "keep his covenant" and his "commandments" (v. 18). God demands that we honor our covenant with him. Although we are saved by grace, that grace will produce in us a worshipful response to God that includes joyful obedience. We are under the New Covenant, but it is still a covenant, and a covenant is a mutual agreement that goes both ways. The New Covenant is a commitment between us and God. Every kind of good relationship involves mutual giving. A relationship is unhealthy if one side always gives and the other side always receives. God himself does not appreciate a relationship in which he gives and gives, but receives nothing in return. God expects us to give something back. What does he want? He wants our hearts; he wants our praise; he wants our love; he wants our worship; he wants our affection. He wants us to worship, honor, and adore him. He wants us to lift him up. He wants us to remember his commandments to do them. We are not saved because we keep the commandments, but we are keeping the commandments because we are saved. We obey God because he saved us. We are saved by the grace of God, but because of the grace of God, we love God, and we want to obey him, we want to please him, we want to serve him, we want to walk with him, we want to be in fellowship with him.

Let every creature bless the Lord.

¹⁹ The LORD has established His throne in heaven,
    And His kingdom rules over all.
²⁰ Bless the LORD, you His angels, Who excel in strength,
    who do His word, Heeding the voice of His word.
²¹ Bless the LORD, all you His hosts,
    You ministers of His, who do His pleasure.
²² Bless the LORD, all His works,
    In all places of His dominion.
    Bless the LORD, O my soul!

As we come to the end of the Psalm we notice a change in focus. The beginning of the Psalm focused on the psalmist himself. He is speaking to himself, encouraging himself to "bless the Lord" for all of his benefits. Then, he moves on to celebrate all that God has done for Israel. Now, he moves beyond himself and Israel to speak of the heavenly hosts. David says, "The Lord has established his throne in heaven, and his kingdom rules over all".

Just as David began the psalm by encouraging himself, "Bless the Lord, O my soul", he now encourages the heavenly hosts and all of God's creatures to "bless the Lord" also. He calls upon the angels, "Bless the Lord". He urges all the hosts of heaven, "Bless the Lord". He challenges all of Gods works, "Bless the Lord". We are reminded of Psalm 148, which also calls for universal praise:

> Praise Him, sun and moon; Praise Him, all you stars of light! Praise Him, you heavens of heavens, And you waters above the heavens! … Praise the LORD from the earth, You great sea creatures and all the depths; Fire and hail, snow and clouds; Stormy wind, fulfilling His word; Moun-

tains and all hills; Fruitful trees and all cedars; Beasts and all cattle; Creeping things and flying fowl; Kings of the earth and all peoples; Princes and all judges of the earth; Both young men and maidens; Old men and children. Let them praise the name of the LORD (Psalm 148:3-13).

After having called upon all of God's creation to bless the Lord, the psalmist turns back to address himself, concluding with the now familiar refrain, "Bless the Lord, O my soul". And let us claim his words for ourselves.

Chapter 10

Praise the Lord!

Psalm 150
[1] Praise the LORD!
>Praise God in His sanctuary;
>Praise Him in His mighty firmament!
[2] Praise Him for His mighty acts;
>Praise Him according to His excellent greatness!
[3] Praise Him with the sound of the trumpet;
>Praise Him with the lute and harp!
[4] Praise Him with the timbrel and dance;
>Praise Him with stringed instruments and flutes!
[5] Praise Him with loud cymbals;
>Praise Him with clashing cymbals!
[6] Let everything that has breath praise the LORD.
>Praise the LORD!

God has called us to praise him. He has saved us and chosen us as his people that we might praise him. He has formed us into the church of the living God in order that we may proclaim the praises of Him who called us out of darkness into his marvelous light (1 Peter 2:9).

>After these things I looked, and behold, a great multitude which no one could number, of all nations, tribes, peoples, and tongues, standing before the throne and before the Lamb, clothed with white robes, with palm branches in their hands, and crying out with a loud voice, saying, Salvation belongs to our God who sits on the throne, and to the Lamb. All the angels stood around the throne and the elders and the four living crea-

tures, and fell on their faces before the throne and worshiped God, saying: Amen! Blessing and glory and wisdom, thanksgiving and honor and power and might, be to our God forever and ever. Amen (Revelation 7:9-12).

Psalm 150 expresses well our ultimate goal of praise, and it serves as a fitting conclusion to the book of Psalms.

The Songs of Praise

As we have said, Psalm 150 is one of the Songs of Praise (also called Hymns). The Songs of Praise normally begin with an invitation to worship, followed by the reason for praise, and conclude with a concluding invitation to worship. Note the following example from Psalms 135 and 113:

1. Call to Worship
   Praise the Lord; Praise the name of the Lord
   Praise him, O you servants of the Lord (135:1)
2. Motive for Worship
   A. God's Majesty
      (1) God's majesty in creation
          Whatever the Lord pleases, he does,
          In heaven and in earth,
          In the seas and in all the deep places (Ps. 135.6)
      (2) God's majesty in his sovereignty
          For I know that the Lord is great,
          And our Lord is above all gods (Ps. 135.5)
   B. God's Love
      (1) God's love in salvation (especially the exodus)
          He destroyed the firstborn of Egypt
          Both of man and beast.
          He sent signs and wonders (Ps. 135.8-9)
      (2) God's love in provision and care
          He raises the poor out of the dust,
          And lifts the needy out of the ash heap (Ps. 113.7)
3. Concluding Call to Worship
   Blessed be the Lord out of Zion,
   Who dwells in Jerusalem!
   Praise the Lord! (Ps. 135.21)

The Hymns teach us to praise God for his unchangeable attributes. He is the God who is majestic and exalted, the King of kings, the Lord of lords, the God of gods. He created the heaven, the earth, the angels, and all of humanity. So let us praise him! Not only is God majestic in his holiness, but he is also loving, kind, and compassionate. He saved Israel from the bondage of Egypt; therefore, let us praise him! The Hymns teach us that the goal of worship is praise. When times are good we should praise God, and when times are bad we should praise God.

Other Hymns include Psalms 24, 29, 33, 46, 48, 50, 67, 68, 75, 76, 81, 82, 90, 100, 105, 107, 113, 114, 115, 117, 124, 125, 129, 134, 135, 136, 147, 149, and 150.

Praise the Lord …

Psalm 150 can be divided into five parts:
1. Invitation to praise (v. 1a) (Call to Worship)
2. Places for praise (v. 1b)
3. Motivation for praise (v. 2) (Motive for Worship)
4. Methods of praise (vv. 3-5)
5. Universal praise (v. 6) (Concluding Call to Worship)

Invitation to praise

[1a] Praise the LORD!

Psalm 150 begins with an invitation to the congregation, "Praise the Lord!". The Hebrew word "praise" is the imperative form of the verb, which suggests a command or an urgent exhortation. "Praise the Lord!" is a call to worship, urging the entire congregation to participate in the praise of the Lord. No one should be a spectator—everyone should praise him.

Who are we praising? The Lord! Who is the Lord? The Lord is Yahweh, traditionally known as Jehovah. He is the God of Abraham, Isaac, and Jacob. He is the God who met Moses at the burning bush in Exodus 3. He said, "Moses, I have come down to deliver my people Israel, to deliver them from the bondage of Egypt and out of the house of slavery and to lead them into a land that flows with milk and honey, the land I promised unto Abraham."

Yahweh, Jehovah, is the God who brought Israel out of bondage, out of slavery. He is Jehovah-Jireh (Genesis 22:14), the Lord who provides. He is Jehovah-Ropheh, the Lord who heals us (Exodus 15:26). He is Jehovah-Shalom, the Lord our peace (Judges 6:24). He is Jehovah-Tsidkenu, the Lord our righteousness (Jeremiah 23:6). He is Jehovah-Nissi, the Lord our banner (Exodus 17:15). He is Yahweh. He is Jehovah. The psalmist did not say praise Allah, or praise Buddha, or praise Krishna—he said, "praise Jehovah". We are invited to come and praise him.

Places of praise

> [1b] Praise God in His sanctuary;
>   Praise Him in His mighty firmament!

The second part of the psalm tells us where we should praise him. First, we should "Praise God in his sanctuary". His "sanctuary" means his "holy place". Here in Psalm 150, the sanctuary probably refers to two locations: God's heavenly abode and his dwelling place in the Jerusalem temple. Therefore, all of the heavenly servants should praise God in heaven, and all of the earthly servants should praise God in the temple. Jesus taught us that where any two or three are gathered together in his name, he is in the midst of them. And wherever Jesus is present, it is a holy place. Wherever God's holy people are gathered together, that is a holy place. It is all about God and his people. Nevertheless, our churches are buildings that are dedicated as a place of worship unto the Lord. Therefore, the church facility is a holy place, a sanctuary that is devoted to God's use.

But the psalmist goes beyond the sanctuary and says, "Praise him in his mighty firmament". In order to understand the word "firmament", we must go back to Genesis, where we read,

> And God said, Let there be a firmament in the midst of the waters, and let it divide the waters from the waters. And God made the firmament, and divided the waters which were under the firmament from the waters which were above the firmament: and it was so. And God called the firmament Heaven. And the evening and the morning were the second day. (Genesis 1:6-8)

On the second day of creation, God divided the waters that were on the surface of the earth (oceans, rivers, and lakes) from the waters that are above the earth (clouds). Clouds are nothing but water vapor, and between the clouds and the earth is the open sky, which Genesis calls "the firmament". It imagines that there is a dome above the sky which holds back the clouds. The sky separates the earth from the clouds. So when he says, "Praise him in his mighty firmament", he means, "Praise him beneath the sky". Wherever we upon the earth and we are able to look up and see the sky, the stars, the sun, the moon, and the clouds, that is a place in which we should praise the Lord. We know that heaven is filled with praise, and heaven lies beyond the firmament, beyond the sky. But here we are told that inside the firmament, inside the circle of the sky, we are to praise God. Whenever we look up and see the stars, let us remember the earlier words of the psalmist: "The heavens declare the glory of God, and the firmament shows forth his handiwork" (Psalm 19:1). Any time we are under the sky, we are in a place of praise. He created the sky with the power of his word, so let us praise him!

Motivation for praise

² Praise Him for His mighty acts;
    Praise Him according to His excellent greatness!

The third section of this Psalm tells us the motive for praise: "praise him for his mighty acts; praise him for his excellent greatness". Jehovah is the God who works and acts on our behalf. He intervenes in our lives. Some people think that God created all things and then stood back to let the world run on its own. But God is very much involved in the world and our lives. Therefore, we come to God in prayer, bringing our needs to the Lord, and we come before God in worship, pouring our hearts to the Lord. The Lord is involved in meeting our needs, hearing our prayers, in working miracles, in directing our steps, and in delivering us daily. "Praise him for his mighty acts". God is neither impotent nor lazy. God is neither detached nor unconcerned. He is powerful and active, and he cares deeply about his people.

The psalmist then says that we should praise God for his attributes: "Praise him according to his excellent greatness". Why should we praise God? Because "Great is the Lord and greatly to be praised" (Psalm 145:3). Praise him because he is great in wisdom. Praise him because he is great in holiness. Praise him because he is great in power. Praise him because he is great in love. Praise him because he is great in faithfulness. Praise him because he is great in his mercy.

Methods of praise

3 Praise Him with the sound of the trumpet;
    Praise Him with the lute and harp!
4 Praise Him with the timbrel and dance;
    Praise Him with stringed instruments and flutes!
5 Praise Him with loud cymbals;
    Praise Him with clashing cymbals!

The fourth section of the Psalm lists the various methods of worship or ways of worship. The psalmist insists that every musical instrument should be used in praising the Lord. Unlike humans, who have preferences for certain musical instruments, God loves to hear every musical instrument used in praising him. The psalmist lists all three kinds of musical instruments: percussion instruments, wind instruments, and stringed instruments. The wind instruments are the trumpets and the pipes. The stringed instruments are the psaltery and the harp. The percussion instruments are the timbrel (tambourine) and the cymbals. He then goes beyond instruments to include the dance. It was common in those days to dance while playing a tambourine. Those of us who cannot play musical instruments can dance unto the Lord. Other physical modes of worship are mentioned in earlier psalms, such as the clapping of hands and shouting.

Our worship services are not meant to be entertainment; they are meant to be offerings unto God. Therefore, our music should be directed toward the Lord as a sacrifice of praise. The New Testament describes our worship as a "sacrifice of praise": "By him therefore let us offer the sacrifice of praise to God continually, that is, the fruit of our lips giving thanks to his name" (Hebrews 13:15). Our participation in worship, whether it be by playing an instrument, clapping our hands, singing, or shouting, should be an offering to the Lord.

Universal praise

⁶ Let everything that has breath praise the LORD.
    Praise the LORD!

Finally, the psalmist tells us that all people should praise God. The invitation to praise is not directed only to the pastor: "All of you pastors, praise the Lord". This invitation to praise is not meant only for church leaders, singers, or the worship team. This invitation is directed at everyone: "Let everything that has breath praise the Lord". Scripture tells us that God breathed into Adam the breath of life (Genesis 2:7) and that God gives breath to every person (Acts 17:25). Let us use that breath to praise God—let everything that has breath praise the Lord. If we look back to Psalm 148, we will find more detail about God's desire for universal praise. The psalmist says, "Praise him all you angels. Praise him all his hosts. The beasts and the cattle, the insects, the birds, praise him. The kings of the earth, the judges, old man, young men, women and children, praise the Lord"—let everything that has breath praise the Lord.

God has given us our breath, and with our breath he gave us the freedom to choose how to use that breath. We can breathe forth blessings or we can breathe forth cursings. We can use our breath to bless God, or we can use our breath to curse God. We can use our breath to injure or to heal, to hurt or to help. We have the choice how we use our breath. Psalm 150 invites us to use our breath in absolute praise! As God breathes into us, we inhale, then as we exhale let it be praise. Every breath that goes forth from our mouth should be praise. Let us not breath out hatred; let us not breath out hurt; let us not breathe out in injury; let us not breathe out envy; let us not breathe forth strife; let us not breathe forth profanity; let us not breathe forth cursing. Rather, let us breathe forth blessing. Let us breathe forth honor. Let us breathe forth praise to the Lord. Let everything that has breath praise the Lord. Let us pray as David prayed, "Let the words of my mouth and the meditations of my heart be acceptable in thy sight, O Lord, my strength and my Redeemer" (Psalm 19:14). Praise ye the Lord. Praise his holy name.

Praise is not an option for us. We must praise him when things are going well, and praise him when things are falling apart. We must praise him when we feel like it and praise them when we do not feel like.

Psalm 150 concludes with a powerful statement of absolute praise. We must come to the place where we can focus entirely upon God and upon giving him praise. We must forget everything else. If we read through the Psalms, we will find plenty of reasons for coming to God with absolute praise:

We have heard that the Lord is our shepherd and we shall not want, so let us praise him.

We have read that he is our rock and our fortress, so let us praise him.

We have heard that the heavens declare the glory of God, so let us praise him.

We have heard that the earth is the Lord's and the fullness thereof, so let us praise him.

We heard that the Lord is our light and our salvation, so let us praise him.

We heard that the Lord brought us up out of a horrible pit, so let us praise him.

We heard that the Lord is our refuge and strength, a very present help in a time of need, so let us praise him.

We have heard that the Lord is good, his mercy is everlasting, and his truth endures to all generations, so let us praise him.

We have heard that he has forgiven all of our sins, so let us praise him.

We also read that he heals all of our diseases, so let us praise him.

We have heard that his greatness is unsearchable, so let us praise him.

We have heard that he will reign as king for ever and for ever, so let us praise him.

We heard that the Lord is coming, so let us praise him.

Let us praise him, not because of a specific answer to prayer, but because of who he is. Let us praise him, not because of just one event when he came to our rescue, but because he is God. Let us praise him because he is Savior, sanctifier, Spirit baptizer, healer, and coming king. Let us praise him because he is worthy to open the book (Revelation 4).

Praise him because he is King of Kings and Lord of lords.

Praise him because he is the Alpha and the Omega. Praise him because he is the Lamb of God takes away the sins of the world.

Praise him because he dwells in the midst of his people.

Praise him because he is a father to the orphan and the husband to the widow.

Praise him because he supplies all of our need.

Praise him for his mighty acts; praise him according to his excellent greatness.

Let everything that has breath praise the Lord.

The Message of the Psalms

The book of Psalms is relevant to every point in our journey of faith. Our every experience finds correspondence either in the praises, the prayers, or the teachings of the book of Psalms. The entire span of worship is encapsulated here in Israel's songbook. In this book of praises, we find also songs of lament and songs of teaching. Every part of the life of faith is explored in the Psalms.

The book of Psalms begins by pronouncing blessings upon the righteous person who delights in the "law of the Lord" and meditates in it "day and night". That person is like a tree planted by the rivers of water that brings forth its fruit in its season, and whatsoever he does will prosper. But the wicked are not so. The wicked are like the husk of the grain that the wind blows away. The wicked cannot stand in the day of judgment, and they do not have a place in the congregation of the righteous. Psalm one concludes by saying that the Lord knows the way of the righteous, but the way of the ungodly will perish.

We begin the book of Psalms, therefore, with a contrast between the righteous and the wicked. The righteous person loves to worship God, and God blesses the worshiper. We do not receive the blessings of God by seeking our own way, by seeking after the things of the world. Jesus said, "Seek first the kingdom of God and his righteousness, and all of these things will be added to you". We are blessed when we seek the word of God, the worship of God and the praise of God. We must come to God with our whole heart to worship him, to meditate in his word, and to walk in his way. If we do this, God will bless us, and he will prosper us.

However, when we get to Psalm 3, we learn that righteous people do not always have it easy. They often encounter opposition in various forms. Therefore, we find psalms of urgent prayer, which we call laments, in which the righteous person cries out to God. In Psalm 13 David prays, "How long? Oh Lord, would you forget me forever? How long, O Lord, will you let me suffer? How long will I endure this pain in my soul?"

These psalms of lament remind us of the story of Job. Even a righteous person like Job—who is perfect, upright, fearing God, and shunning evil—will suffer. He was a righteous man, yet God allowed a testing time in his life. The Psalms show us that during times of testing the psalmist would cry out to God, and plead for God's help. We also go through those kinds of experiences. When we are in the midst of the valley, the way to get out of the valley is to bow our knees before the Lord, pour out our hearts to God, and worship him wholeheartedly. We must not ignore God when we are in the valley. We must not avoid the church when we are suffering. Many people make the mistake of trying to face their problems alone. But when we are in trouble that is when we really need the church. The church is where we can pray. The church is where brothers and sisters will intercede for us. We need one another when we are in trouble. We must not shut out people when we are in trouble. We need to allow them to help us when we are at the time of trouble.

In our times of trouble we can go to the Psalms and find examples of how we should seek the face of God. What happens when we pray? God answers. In answer to our prayers God sends blessings. In answer to our prayers God sends healings. In answer to our prayers God sends miracles. As we read through the Psalms, we find prayers, then we find Psalms of Thanksgiving.

In the Psalms of Thanksgiving, the psalmist gives thanks to God his answers to prayer. An example of the Psalm of Thanksgiving is Psalm 40, in which the psalmist testifies of God's saving power. He "cried unto the Lord" in the midst of his trouble, and God "inclined" to him and heard his cry. God bent down to listen, then he lifted him up out of the horrible pit, out of the mirey clay, and he set his feet upon a rock. We could also point to Psalm 107, in which those who wandered in the wilderness cried unto the Lord, and the Lord heard their cry, and he delivered them from all their troubles. Therefore, we should "praise the Lord for his goodness and for his wonderful works unto the children of men". Those who were sick and afflicted cried to God, and God sent his word and healed them. Therefore, we should praise him.

So the book of Psalms begins with a call to righteousness and worship. Then it moves on to the psalms of prayer, in which the psalmist relates a time of deep suffering and pain. Out of that pain, the psalmist cries to God for help. When God answers the psalmist's prayers, a song of thanksgiving is offered. In addition to the praises that are offered in response to a specific time of deliverance, the book of Psalms records hymns of praise that exalt the Lord for his nature and attributes.

This progression, however, is not a simple step-by-step process that begins with teaching, leads to prayer, and ends in praise. Psalm 40 begins with praise and ends with prayer. The life of faith is not the same every day. The Christian life is not all sorrow, and it is not all joy. We go through trials of our faith, tests, opposition, and troubles. But the Christian life is not all testing and trouble—God gives us deliverance and God gives us joy. As the psalmist said, "Weeping may endure for a night, but joy comes in the morning" (Psalm 30:5).

The book of Psalms concludes with a series of four hymns of praise. These last four psalms bring us to a whole new level of praise. Psalms 147-150 encourage us to praise God for his character and his attributes. These last few psalms might be called psalms of absolute praise. In the hymns of praise, the focus of the attention is no longer on our prayers and how God answered us but the emphasis is upon God, his nature, his holiness, his power, his majesty, his love, and his grace. The praise is focused entirely upon God and his nature and purposes and work.

Absolute praise

Psalm 150 is the greatest example of absolute praise, and its placement at the end of the Psalter points to the fact that our goal as God's people is to worship God completely. As we journey with God, we live before him, pray unto him, our give thanks unto him.

We experience the ups and downs of life and sometimes seem to be going nowhere. However, Psalm 150 teaches us that we have one goal and we are headed in one direction—our goal is the place of absolute praise. One day, every knee will bow before him, and every tongue will confess that Jesus Christ is Lord, to the glory of God the father (Philippians 2:10-11). We are moving towards the day when everything in heaven will praise God, everything in the earth will praise God, and everything under the earth will praise the name of the Lord. Every part of creation will give praise and glory to God (Revelation 5:11-14). Our goal is a time and a place where there will be no more sun because the son of God will be the light. And God's city, the holy city, new Jerusalem, will come down from God out of heaven, and the city will be in the midst of his people, and God will dwell in the midst of us, he will be the temple. We will live and remain in his presence to glorify and praise him for ever and ever.

Praise is our goal

We are on a journey; and though, like Abraham, we travel to a place that we have never seen before, we do not wander aimlessly. We seek for the city "whose builder and maker is God" (Hebrews 11:10). We await the return of Jesus, and we look for the presence of God to come down out of heaven and his kingdom to be established. God himself is the beginning and the end, and our goal is to reach the place of absolute praise.

More than any other psalm, Psalm 150 eloquently expresses our goal of praise. It is the only psalm that includes the word "praise" in every line—thirteen times "praise" is encouraged. This is the place of absolute praise to which God wants to bring us. This is the place of absolute praise that will bring fulfillment to our lives. This is the place of absolute praise that will bear witness to the fact that we are mature as Christians. This is the place of absolute praise that brings us into God's presence, whether it be at home, whether it be at church, or whether we be standing on the street corner. Absolute praise is when we can lift our voices to God, and we are not thinking about who we are or what our needs are, but we are thinking only of who God is and how wonderful it is to have him as the Lord of our lives. We lift up our voices to praise him and magnify him because of his greatness, because of his love, because of his mercy, because he is God and we are not God. We need to come to that place of maturity of praise where we can lift our voices to the Lord and say, "O Lord, it is you Lord. It is all about you. We come to worship you. O Lord we are here to praise you, hallelujah! Lord, let us forget about ourselves, and our needs, and our circumstances, and let us just praise the name of the Lord.

In the New Testament, we are called to absolute praise by the Apostle Paul who writes, "Rejoice in the Lord always. Again I will say, rejoice!" (Philippians 4:4), and "to him be glory in the church … forever and ever"(Ephesians 3:21)). John envisioned a day when God's people would be enveloped in absolute praise. He writes,

> After these things I looked, and behold, a great multitude which no one could number, of all nations, tribes, peoples, and tongues, standing before the throne and before the Lamb, clothed with white robes, with palm branches in their hands, and crying out with a loud voice, saying, "Salvation belongs to our God who sits on the throne, and to the Lamb!" All the angels stood around the throne and the elders and the four living creatures, and fell on their faces before the throne and worshiped God, saying: "Amen! Blessing and glory and wisdom, thanksgiving and honor and power and might, be to our God forever and ever. Amen. (Revelation 7:9-12)

There is difference in status or rank among the heavenly multitude. Every person has equal access to the presence of God. One is not better than the other, but all are standing before the throne of God with palm branches in their hands and the praises of God on their lips. This is the kind of praise to which Psalm 150 calls us. We must pattern our worship after the worship of heaven. We must come to the place where we forget ourselves and get lost in his praises. We must become immersed in praise like David, who "danced before the Lord with all his might" (2 Samuel 6:14) and like John who "was in the Spirit on the Lord's day" (Revelation 1:10).

Psalm 150 exemplifies that kind of praise—total, absolute praise, where we are surrendered into the presence of God and we worship him in spirit and in truth. Most of the world seeks for joy through entertainment, hobbies, and diversions. They go out to eat, watch a movie, go to the beach, play golf, hang out in clubs and bars, or watch TV. These leisure activities are ways of finding peace and joy in life. Many of them are helpful and acceptable, but they cannot replace worship, because it is in worship that we find our greatest fulfillment. We were created to worship God. We were created to have fellowship with God. We were created to know God, to love God, and to worship God with absolute praise.

Bibliography for Study of the Psalms

Allen, Leslie C., *Psalms* (Word Biblical Themes; Waco, Tex.: Word Books, 1987).

Bonhoeffer, Dietrich, and Eberhard Bethge, *Psalms: The Prayer Book of the Bible* (Minneapolis,: Augsburg Pub. House, 1970).

Brueggemann, Walter, *The Message of the Psalms : A Theological Commentary* (Augsburg Old Testament Studies; Minneapolis: Augsburg Pub. House, 1984).

Bullock, C. Hassell, *Encountering the Book of Psalms : A Literary and Theological Introduction* (Encountering Biblical Studies; Grand Rapids, MI: Baker Academic, 2001).

Eaton, J. H., *Psalms: Introduction and Commentary* (Torch Bible Commentaries; London,: S. C. M. Press, 1967).

Goldingay, John, *Psalms* (Baker Commentary on the Old Testament Wisdom and Psalms; 3 vols.; Grand Rapids, MI: Baker Academic, 2006).

Limburg, James, *Psalms* (Westminster Bible Companion; Louisville, KY: Westminister John Knox Press, 1st edn, 2000).

Mays, James Luther, *Psalms* (Interpretation; Louisville, KY: John Knox Press, 1994).

Sarna, Nahum M., *Songs of the Heart : An Introduction to the Book of Psalms* (New York: Schocken Books : Distributed by Pantheon Books, 1st edn, 1993).

Wilcock, Michael, *The Message of Psalms: Songs for the People of God* (Bible Speaks Today; 2 vols.; Downers Grove, IL: InterVarsity Press, 2001).

17157503R00099

Made in the USA
Charleston, SC
29 January 2013